Get

The title of Tony's book is very apt. He has had at least three lives, and each one of them has been rich and engrossing. His experience as a policeman and with the Deep Sea Mission clearly prepared him for the extraordinary ministry that he and his heroic wife Ruth exercised in Battersea for so many difficult and rewarding years. Tony writes with such humour and passion about the different strands of his life that readers are sure to be entertained and inspired by the narrative. I commend this book to all who value reality and straightforwardness in faith.

Adrian Plass, Writer and International Speaker

I have known Tony since his Shaftesbury Christian Centre days over ten years ago and loved reading 'Get a Life'. His stories are vivid, often very amusing, accounts of real-life people – deeply inspiring and moving for all, particularly perhaps for those who share to any extent God's care, concern and love for the poor.

Rt. Rev'd. Sandy Millar, Bishop in the Province of Uganda
Assistant Bishop in London, Vicar Tottington Parish

One of my first encounters with Tony was way back in the mid 1980s, taking a missionary team to work with him and the Church in the Shaftesbury Christian Centre in Battersea. Whilst many Christians were making their way to the suburbs, Tony and Ruth were committed to the inner city and 'Get a Life' is their story and it comes with a challenge to us all.

Steve Clifford, General Director of Evangelical Alliance

I have known Tony Powell for over 50 years. His life of radical obedience to God totally gives the lie to the idea that Christianity is boring. His willingness to respond to the next challenge from heaven has resulted in him becoming a lifelong adventurer. If this book does not challenge and inspire you then you're in trouble. In fact, I suspect you may already be dead! Read it and savour it. It will give you a taste for a life out of the ordinary. There is a very real risk that you yourself will become as radical for Jesus as Tony has always been. You cannot fail to be encouraged when you read that this man has lived with a lifelong struggle to believe in himself. It's just as well he discovered a God who believed in him even if he didn't believe in himself. Thanks Tony for a life of faith and for years of friendship.

Eric Delve, Vicar of St. Luke's Church, Maidstone, Leader of Detling Bible Week

It has been my privilege to know Tony and Ruth as friends for many years. This is their story told in their own inimitable way. It will make you laugh and cry, it is the story of two ordinary people who dared to believe God and His promises and to live in His faithfulness. They listened and obeyed and are honest enough - as I would expect them to be - to tell it how it really was! Their journey has been one of faith in Him who never fails and in following Him they discovered their destiny.

Norman Barnes, Founder of Links International

Get a Life

Tony Powell

RoperPenberthy Publishing

Published by RoperPenberthy Publishing Ltd, Springfield House,
23 Oatlands Drive, Weybridge, Surrey KT13 9LZ

ISBN 978-1-903905-67-8

Cover design by Audri Coleman

Printed in England by Cox & Wyman Ltd, Reading

DEDICATIONS

Most especially to my beloved wife for her unfailing support, encouragement and love throughout our fifty-two years of marriage.

Then to our children Tina, Clifford and Richard whose love and support throughout our many changes of homes, schools and friends, have always been there for us. We thank God for Bill, Kym and Mary who now share their lives. They all mean so much to us.

Finally our grandchildren, Carol, Alex, Zoe and Thomas; Helen, Rachel and Robert; Conor and Joshua. I hope you enjoy 'Papa's stories', "Get A Life".

Tony Powell, 2010

Contents

Chapter 1

Beginnings

"Let's see your appointments men," said the duty sergeant at Wandsworth police station. Six officers produced their pocket book, whistle, truncheon and torch. To them it was just another night duty. It was all new to me. My beat covered the dingy street behind the gasworks and this was my first night duty in Wandsworth. I was the new probation constable straight from Hendon Police College and was feeling intimidated by the experienced men standing in line with me. "It's a quiet night for you all tonight, apart from .... " The sergeant went on to give information about stolen cars and local issues. Most of the men seemed to ignore what he was saying but I was desperately trying to remember every word. The parade room was located in the basement of the police station. It was as cold and as uninviting as the streets outside. The sergeant leaned against the well-worn wooden lectern and mentioned something about the Police Federation. Behind him was a door leading to the cells along the corridor. He was about to dismiss us for the night's duty when the door slowly opened and a little elderly man appeared holding a small packet. To my horror it was my dad. "I've got your sandwiches, Tony," he said and waved them in my direction. I groaned inwardly. "Dad, you can't do this to me." Then silence. This room was out of bounds to the public. The sergeant raised his eyebrows. "What have we got here?" he asked. A few sniggers were heard in the ranks. I dare not walk up to him and take them; I just couldn't do it. I felt rooted to the spot. "Okay, leave 'em there," said the sergeant with a sigh, and pointed to a pile of newspapers. With a smile and a wave dad disappeared down the corridor. All I could say to myself was, "I know you love me dad, and thanks for coming out late at night but never, never do that again." Four hours later, feeling like a cat that had been locked out, I returned to the station for sandwiches and a hot drink. Thanks dad, I love you. But ....

We lived in a large five-bedroomed house called Ormond Lodge in Poplar Grove, New Malden, Surrey. It was spacious and at times rather careworn. All my childhood memories are happy ones. Our parents had the daunting task of raising a family of four during the second world war. Mother did not enjoy the best of health and needed help to run the household. Food was basic with much of it produced in the large garden, which contained chickens, bees, ducks and rabbits. Washing machines and refrigerators were not to be seen in our home till many years later. The family wash took place every Monday and all the clothes were boiled in a tub in the kitchen and then put through the mangle. The kitchen filled with steam and the condensation ran in rivers down the window. Water spilled onto the tiled floor as one of the four children turned the handle of the mangle. Dad had a Rayburn installed in the kitchen which gave hot water to the house and also powered the one radiator in the hall. Open fires heated the dining room and lounge, and coal and coke were delivered by the ton every winter. Huge lumps of coal were burnt in the lounge fireplace and I loved to see the smoke hiss out of the coal and then ignite into flames of blue, red and white. There was no heating in the bedrooms and the winter months caused the condensation on the inside of the window panes to freeze into beautiful patterns of ice. Rationing during the war years restricted children to six pennyworth of sweets a week, which we all bought at our local shop, Formans, in Elm Grove, New Malden.

We all started our school days at the local Church of England Infants' School in Lime Grove. The Headmistress was called Miss Speading. I was the third child in the family to attend this school. It was an old Victorian stone building looking like a church. The corridor walls were lined with hooks on which I hung my dark navy blue raincoat. We sat in individual desks with holes for ink pots. The walls were bare; I can't remember any pictures. A huge glass screen divided us from the class next door. The teachers used flash cards to teach us the alphabet. I don't recall any fun or games apart from the usual playtime. One day, the teacher asked the children to stand if they attended the local Anglican Sunday school. Most stood. I remained seated. I felt alone and worried about what she might say to those still seated. Finally she walked over and coldly asked, "Where do you go then?" I didn't know what our church was called, so I mumbled, "I think it's called 'The Hall'." Certainly my parents always referred to it as, 'The Hall'. I just hated being different from all the class and no doubt blushed. "Well," she said in a harsh voice, "where is it then?" All I could mumble out with my head down was, "It's a long way, Miss, and we all go every Sunday."

I felt humiliated in front of the class. Her attitude cut me to the heart. For the first time in life I knew what it was like to be alone. Perhaps a foretaste of the 'Narrow Way' Jesus once spoke about – an experience to be encountered many times in life. In fact, I loved going to 'The Hall'. Every Sunday our parents and we four children would walk hand in hand three times a day to 'The Hall'. We seemed to take up the width of the road. There were few cars on the road then.

After Lime Grove Infants I moved onto Elm Road Junior School and I remember being with a group of boys, one of whom was bragging about his 'five bob' (25p) a week from a paper round. "Wow, that's a pound a month," I said to myself. "In ten months I could buy a new bike." I imagined myself walking out of the village shop pushing a brand new racing bike. It made my sixpence (2½p) a week look pathetic. It soon became known in the family that Tony was on a mission, I was daily pestering newspaper shops for work. My dream of riches didn't last long. Father said, "No." I had to learn that such an occupation was below our 'station in life'. Seeing my disappointment he offered me work in the garden and promised to double my pocket money. I didn't realise that social standing was an important issue in suburbia. He later would correct me if I said I was going to work. His reply was, "No, Tony, you go to business." Yet at heart he was never a snob – far from it – for our home was open to all. I think his Victorian attitude came from his parents. All this changed when war broke out; old attitudes and values disappeared along with many of London's houses. Looking back, I don't think early rising for a paper round would have lasted more than a week. Of course, father knew that, and after all, a shilling (5p) a week wasn't bad for a small boy.

Every year, the entire school marched to the Anglican church for an Easter service. One year, I decided to take my pet white mouse with me and had it secure in my blazer pocket. I now have no idea why I wanted to do this, but little boys do that sort of thing. Needless to say, sitting through sermons was not my idea of fun so I let it run over my hands and fingers until it finally escaped up my sleeve. Soon it was wriggling its way out of my collar at the back of my neck. The scream that came from the teacher behind me was followed by my being summarily escorted to the exit. My love for white mice was not appreciated by the form mistress.

The school was only a few minutes' walk from my home, so I returned home for my midday meal. However, my friends stayed for school dinners. Although I pestered my mother for school dinners, she adamantly refused, saying it was a waste of money. The cost for a week's dinner was two shillings and a penny (11p). Being a determined little chap, I found a way of raising the money. My brother had a wooden sailing boat with red sails; we often sailed it on the Beverly Park lake. It was a beauty. The thought came to me that I could pawn this at the second-hand shop in Elm Grove to pay for my school dinners. No sooner the thought than the deed. Soon I was walking out of the shop with two shillings and sixpence in my hand (12$\frac{1}{2}$p). All this was unknown to my dear parents. Next Monday I duly paid my money for the week's dinners. The teacher was a little puzzled as to why I only wanted them for a week. I said nothing, but mother had to be told. The outcome of it was that I enjoyed the week's dinners and extra playtime with my friends but my pocket money was stopped to redeem the boat.

Dad often took me fishing on the River Thames. I loved these occasions. His objective was to catch fish for food. Unfortunately, they tasted like the river they were caught in. Never mind – they were great times. I loved watching the big steamers that made trips from Hampton Court Bridge to Kingston and back. We often fished near Hampton Court Bridge. One Bank Holiday, the river banks were crowded with holidaymakers, some of whom were bathing in the river, while others enjoyed the sun. The bathers were told by dad to "Clear off." He wanted to catch his supper. One enterprising old man was selling ice cream from a huge metal tub in a rowing boat. It was a hot day and he was doing a roaring trade. As he got nearer to our fishing area I was hoping dad would buy me one. To my dismay dad said, "Sorry Tony; do you see what he is doing?" Well, no I didn't. "Just you watch him then," he said. Then even to my amazement I saw that after each scoop of ice cream he washed the metal scoop in the muddy river. Health and safety was much less of an issue in those far-off days. No doubt there were many sore tummies that night.

Christmas time was always a very special time in the family. We never went to a Christmas service, for every Sunday was a celebration of my parents' faith. My memories are of Christmas stockings, presents, parties and relations filling the house, big log fires, chicken dinners, the parson's nose, the wishbone, home-made Christmas crackers (with no crack), and most important of all, charades. This was followed by what was known as 'dad's initiation test'. It was the craziest of games, one of his own invention, never to be repeated in family life again. He would tell us not to leave the front room until the signal was given. He would then leave and prepare an obstacle route around our large house. Stair rods would be removed from the stairs carpet, and chairs suspended on ropes would dangle over the staircase. Tables were turned upside down, and near them were placed wet blankets and sometimes a bowl of chicken guts! A trip wire that would turn the vacuum cleaner on, a few sprigs of holly scattered about and the ghostly noises he made all added to the fun. He would return to the living room, turn all the lights out and tell us the course had to be completed on our hands and knees and the destination was the bathroom at the far end of the house. Children loved it, but I am sure mother groaned within as she knew the work necessary to return the house back into shape for the next day. She was very patient, and no doubt relieved that no bones were broken because of her husband's crazy ideas. Christmas was fun.

School days were often interrupted by air raids. Multiplication tables were learned in the air raid shelters. En route to school we picked up shrapnel and if I found a piece with brass on it then I knew I was in for a good swap with another boy. I am told that during one heavy raid over New Malden, mother asked how we were coping. My reply was, "My nerve is a little cracked." Maybe it was that reply that made my parents decide to evacuate to Cornwall, which was very wise as a few days later several people in our street were killed in another bombing raid.

I have wonderful memories of staying in an old farmhouse in Pendoggett. The farmer allowed me to ride the horse as it pulled the old cart around the farm. Chickens ran in the muddy yard, and he also kept a few pigs. It was an old-fashioned farm. I have never forgotten the smell of barns filled with hay. For me it was heaven, but not for mother. We all went down with German measles and flea bites and the doctors advised her to get out as soon as possible. The nearest village to us was Port Isaac, several miles from the farm. We made our way there by following a small stream that ran through Happy Valley. It was a magical walk – tall yellow iris flags grew alongside the banks, and red toadstools and violets on the banks. It was perfect. We enjoyed taking daring leaps across the stream, no doubt getting very wet at times. When we returned home in the evening we caught fireflies and put them in bottles. All in all a far cry from the bombed streets of London.

During our time in Cornwall, dad continued to work and live at the bank in the City of London. At night time, he was on the roof of the bank watching out for fire bombs. He did this in three-week shifts and on the fourth week he would visit us in Cornwall for a few days. My parents both had to cope with a lot of stress but as a child I felt secure and enjoyed life. After a while there was a let-up in the bombing and we returned to New Malden and school.

We lived with a strong work ethic at home. We all had to be doing something which in general had to be 'useful'. I believe in her heart mother wanted all of us to be missionaries. In many ways we all were at different stages of our lives. Church meetings took up a lot of mother's time. She was a popular speaker. She also produced and edited The Friendly Magazine in which she serialised the family stories she wrote during her lifetime. It also featured devotional articles and poems written by her many friends and admirers. It had a circulation of two thousand. For relaxation she enjoyed outings to London. It gave her great pleasure to catch the Green Line bus to Knightsbridge and spend time in Derry and Toms shop, taking afternoon tea on the rooftop garden. She often bought curtain material there. Jennifer, my sister, accompanied her on these trips, but for some reason I didn't.

The house was always bursting with visitors, many staying for a considerable time. Most were missionaries on leave, or else distant relations passing through London. Fortunately, mum had domestic help in the home in the shape of Mrs. Pepperel. I recall she took pity on our cat that was only fed from the scraps of food left over from our table. I also remember Miss Stevens, who had awful rubber lips and wanted to kiss me. This did not go down well with a little boy.

Dad ran the teenage club for boys at the 'Gospel Hall'. Most of the lads were from poor homes in the district and came for the free tea, sandwiches, and table tennis. Over the years I developed into a good table tennis player and could beat most of them. This became a real problem to me as I didn't want in any way to belittle them in front of their friends, so I often chose to lose the game. I felt this stood me in good stead with them all. I've never been very competitive – perhaps it goes back to those days. The evening always closed with a few rousing hymns and a short talk. It was held in a small side room. Soon the effect of hot tea and sandwiches began to work through their systems, and suppressed groans and smells soon filled the room. Dad ignored all this and continued with his talk. What a man! He loved every minute of it. I shall never forget the time when dad invited a visitor to talk to the lads. He launched into a lengthy prayer. Carried away with his thoughts, he was unaware that the lads were leaving the room one by one. When he finished his prayer, my father and I were the only ones left in the room. I had to suppress my laughter. Dad was full of apologies. What a night!

I had a special friend called Peter Smy. He lived at the end of our road and we spent countless hours together in the grounds of the derelict manor house opposite our home in Poplar Grove. The spacious grounds were full of very climbable trees and overgrown gardens. Over the years the house had been vandalised and stripped of anything of value. It was also the home of a gang of twelve-year-olds who lived nearby. Our favourite occupation was building dens hidden away from the public footpath that made its way between Chestnut Grove and Poplar Grove. We put a lot of work into this den. We dug three feet into the earth, covered it with a sheet of corrugated iron and managed to push an old cast-iron pipe through the roof as a chimney which was attached to a biscuit tin which served as our cooking stove. We then covered the roof with soil and branches, not wanting the rival gang to know of our whereabouts. We loved every minute of being hidden away in a den only known to us. The plan was to have an early morning breakfast cooked on our own underground stove. We arranged to do this at 6am, well before anyone else in the house was awake. I was to provide the eggs and bacon and Peter the matches, frying pan and sticks. The big question was how would I wake up at six in the morning. Peter said it would be no trouble for him as he had an alarm clock. I did not have one. So we came up with the idea that I should tie a string around my big toe, the end of which would be in a bush twenty feet below my bedroom window. Peter would give it a couple of tugs and wake me up. So far so good. I went to sleep looking forward to the eggs and bacon which I had hidden under my bed. Suddenly I found myself in unbearable pain. I felt as if my toe was about to be pulled off. I could not reach the light switch to give the signal that I was awake. He pulled and pulled, and soon I found myself hopping across the bedroom until my foot shot out of the open window. I dare not scream, knowing it would wake everyone in the house, which would have spoilt the whole plan. Mum did not know about the eggs and bacon under my bed for one thing. Seeing my leg out of the window, he gave a wave and said, "Are you awake? I thought you would never get up. Why didn't you turn the light on?" I was in too much pain to reply. Fortunately it didn't stop our fry-up, although our biscuit tin didn't do a very good job. The bacon wouldn't fry and if I remember rightly the eggs were a dirty colour as a result of the entire den being filled with smoke. Early morning commuters to the City, using the nearby footpath, must have been amused to see two ten-year-olds holding a frying pan full of blackened contents and smoke rising from a pile of twigs and a rusty drain pipe.

The rival gang led by Billy Allen caught me alone one afternoon in the Manor House. This was their territory and they were going to punish me for entering their headquarters. They were several years older than me and were going to make sure I would never enter their territory again. They pushed me upstairs and forced me through an open window. The slates on the roof had been removed and provided a sort of ladder that went to the top of the roof. "Up you go or else," they said, and put a fist in my face. Suddenly I was scared; this was serious. One slip and .... "Go, I told you, go," he said. I often climbed trees but I had never been on a roof. I was frightened. Slowly I made my way to the roof followed by Billy Allen. Once on top, I straddled the roof and edged along the pinnacle of the roof to a tree at the far end. "That's your way down and we will be waiting for you at the bottom." I had twenty feet to cover as I eased my way along the hot slates that burnt my hands and legs. Fortunately, the branches of the tree were close to the roof top and climbing down wasn't a problem. Looking back on this incident now it sends a shiver down my spine. I returned home trembling and exhausted. Dad was livid, he knew the Allens. I don't know what he said to them but their gang never troubled us again.

The local authority had other plans for the grounds of the Manor House. It was to be the site for twelve council houses. Soon the house was demolished and a new road built called Fairmead Close. All this happened towards the end of the war. My sister Jennifer discovered that German prisoners of war had been drafted in to build the road. She told my mother who felt sorry for the workmen and sent Jennifer over to them with a tray of tea. She rushed back to the house saying, "They are all Germans and their names are Frits, Nits and Stephen." Within a short time they became great friends with Jennifer and soon she was running errands to Bashfords, the local greengrocers, buying sweets and goodies for them. Soon after that we heard the final 'All Clear' telling us the war was over.

During the summer months, we ate our meals in the garden. On one occasion Grandma Powell joined us for afternoon tea. It was an important event for dad, for this was the only time that I can recall her visiting us. Unfortunately the garden chair collapsed under her weight and she finished up under the table. Dad was horrified – the look on his face said it all. Everyone rushed to help. He was the youngest of seven children; his brothers had all done well in business – one was a London Magistrate. I think the invitation to tea was meant to impress his mother. I know we all had to be on our best behaviour. She was a lovely lady and laughed off this unfortunate event. Conversation was resumed and we finished off our tea.

Dad seemed to have little interest in the house. His focus was the garden – his ducks, vegetables, gooseberry bushes, pear, apple and plum trees. Sometimes he kept rabbits and on one occasion a small pike in a water tank. His main concern was to produce food for the family. He enjoyed giving us wheelbarrow rides at high speed around the garden and tipping us out onto piles of leaves. His hobby was beekeeping. He had five hives, and during summer evenings if he was missing in the home, mother would say, "Go and find dad," and we knew where he would be – watching the activity around the hives. Honey extraction was always a great event and we were expected to help even if we suffered the occasional sting. Stings didn't seem to bother him. On one occasion he showed me a bee sting moving in circles on the back of his hand. "Never squeeze the sting, Tony," he said. "Just flick it out because if you squeeze a sting it injects the poison into the hand." He would then flick the sting out, give his hand a rub and continue turning the extractor handle.

As the years went by, I discovered he held very strong views. Some people said that talking to him was like hitting a brick wall. Mother was prepared to talk issues through but I didn't take the opportunity to do so. I had a long way to go before I was ready for discussions with adults. My life at this time was dominated by football, bike rides, and climbing trees.

The only occupation that dad ever considered was working for the bank. Laurie, my older brother, started work there followed by Madeline, my older sister. In due course I had to follow on. I was certainly not qualified for such a job, but dad pulled a few strings, saying that the bank would be a good and safe introduction to life. I soon found myself in Barclays head office being interviewed by a sombre-looking old man in a serious suit sitting behind a big mahogany desk. I was also wearing an uncomfortable suit. He asked me what paper I read, no doubt expecting me to reply that I took the Times or the Daily Express. I could only think of the Mirror, and even then I realised that this would not be acceptable in his circle. However, I was accepted into the safe arms of Barclays Bank and there I stayed for the next two years.

I worked in the head office, which necessitated visiting the city banks. It was the best place to be as a young man. This again was dad's idea and I thank him for it. There were a dozen or so other lads about the same age in the bank which made life more enjoyable. I was given the nickname of Moses when they discovered I was reading his life story. I worked a five-and-a-half-day week, was paid very little, ran a motor bike and had lots of fun with friends.

My boyhood friend was David Bendell. He didn't share my enthusiasm for motor bikes; he had more sense than to waste his money on the sort of old wrecks that I rode around on. However, that didn't spoil a friendship that went back to the days when we were in short trousers. Looking back, we seem to have attended an endless round of church meetings. The spiritual content of these meetings was not the focus of our interest but rather the fun of being together and meeting up with friends. We both recall going to hear a well-known missionary from China called Gladys Aylward. She was speaking in a huge marquee in Worcester Park in Surrey. We sat in the back row behind a gentleman whose upturned trilby hat sat on the grass beside his chair.

Towards the end of the meeting there was a heavy downpour of rain and unfortunately the old marquee leaked in several places around his chair. With a few sly movements of footwork we managed to manoeuvre his trilby under the drips of water and watched as it gently filled to the brim. I cannot remember the outcome of this sad event. However the missionary was a fiery preacher and challenged everyone to consider the 'mission field' as she called it. She later became internationally known for taking hundreds of children on an epic march over Chinese mountains to escape the Japanese during the second world war. Several years later, Hollywood made a film of this heroic event called the 'Inn of the Sixth Happiness', the role of Miss Aylward was taken by Ingrid Bergman, a film star who bore little resemblance to the tiny four-foot-nothing missionary. Gladys wore a traditional Chinese pigtail tight around her pale face and preached with passion on that wet afternoon in Worcester Park. Although we were lads at the time, maybe she influenced us without us realising it at the time. We both later became involved in missionary work. David many years later directed a missionary enterprise called Emmanuel International and I did what I did. Sorry about the trilby, Sir, I hoped you looked before you put it on.

During the summer months a children's mission was held on Wimbledon Common. It was led by Arthur Page, who was known to everyone as 'Uncle Arthur'. He thoroughly enjoyed singing energetic action choruses along with the children. The event attracted a good number of church teenagers and proved to be a good meeting place for young romantics. It also gave the lads a chance to show off their skills at 'crocker', a local version of rounders. Hundreds of children from local housing estates enjoyed the games, races, food and Bible stories. During the last week I found myself talking more and more to a radiant happy girl from Bexhill called Ruth. We soon started taking evening walks across the common together, enjoying every moment of each other's company. Little did I know that her father had told her not to talk to any London boys. She was lovely to be with and I thought she had an eye for me. After the final meeting I offered to take her to the bus stop. Having my bike handy, in view of the long walk I offered her the use of the crossbar. Somewhere along the common path I hit a pothole and the next we knew we were lying in the middle of a prickly bush with the bike on top of us. I honestly didn't plan this, but it was fun. Soon it was time to say goodbye. As the bus pulled away I cycled after it calling out, "When shall we see each other again?" The reply was, "The Union." Thinking she meant a pub in

Kingston I toured the entire town to find it, but without success. I later learned she said, "Reunion" by which she meant the Mission Reunion in Westminster Central Hall.

Young love has its ways and we found ourselves sitting together at the reunion, more interested in each other than the proceedings up front. Ruth recalled that after the meeting we sat on a bench in Trafalgar Square. We then walked to Victoria Station and said our goodbyes. Although feeling a lot of affection for each other, we only managed a little handshake and a sad cheerio. Within a short time Ruth left her family in Bexhill and moved to New Malden, finding employment in Barclays Bank in the City.

Now dressed as a city slicker, complete with high heels, rolled umbrella, slinky black skirt and looking very confident, she walked along Lombard Street in the City. She was now no longer a schoolgirl but a bank secretary. She quickly attracted the attention of several workmen on a building site who whistled at her. Full of embarrassment she tripped, her high heel got caught in a drain cover and both she and her umbrella went flying. Picking herself up she had a little chuckle to herself and carried on as though nothing had happened. At heart she was a sporty, happy girl, full of love and fun and I was just a lad of seventeen.

Our lives really centred around church events; pop music hadn't arrived and what was current such as Donald Peers was of no interest to us. Elvis and the Beatles arrived when we were in our twenties but again they made a minimal impact on our lives. We really enjoyed visits to the 'pictures' (cinema) as it was called then. 'Ben Hur' made Ruth disappear under her seat, as she could not watch the violent scenes of chariot racing. I loved it all.

Ruth's passion was the athletics track while mine was motor bikes. We both earned around £4 a week. £1 went on a season ticket to the city and another £1 for our keep at home. I loved motor bikes and looked with utter envy on the new gleaming models, with my favourite being the Matchless 350 scrambler bike. I could never afford such a luxury, having to settle for an old Francis Barnet 125 with a hand change gearstick on the side of the petrol tank. It cost me £10. I remember how the red knob broke off from the gearstick and the sharp jagged metal end tore a huge hole in one of my motor cycle gloves. The gloves were made by my mother from an old sheepskin rug. Helmets were not compulsory in those days, thank goodness, as I don't think I could have afforded one.

My next bike was a 250 Velocette and then finally I became the proud owner of a 350 ex-WD Royal Enfield. This I bought from James Sully for £17. However, I lost interest in the bike after badly injuring my foot in an accident so I sold it back to him for the same amount. One great joy was seeing my friends standing at the side of the road to watch me ride flat out at 40 mph. My head would be touching the handlebars, while an old cut-out gas mask strapped to my head served as goggles. My friends would wave and cheer as I would tear past in a cloud of smoke and dust. All great fun. My bikes were all old bangers, not capable of high speeds and constantly breaking down. Were this not the case, I might not be here to tell the tale. My longest trip was to Margate to visit dad's mother; he rode pillion. I remember the police stopped us en route;

dad was also wearing a cut-out gas mask. We must have looked a comical sight. I think he explained to them that he was supporting his son's enthusiasm. Their only concern was that we would arrive in one piece, which fortunately we did.

Ruth joined the Barclays Bank Sports Club and from time to time I watched her in competition. On one special occasion she was running for the bank at the White City Stadium. I managed to get on the track pretending to be her trainer. I don't think my dedication was appreciated by Ruth and I was promptly sent back to the stands. She took athletics seriously and trained regularly in the local parks.

In 1954 the entire church was stirred by the arrival of Billy Graham for the Crusade at Haringey Arena. Huge posters appeared all over London. The press gave him front-page coverage but they were not happy about this flamboyant American preacher who was daring to tell the Brits how to live. My enthusiasm was totally ignited by the whole event. He became a superhero to me. I was part of a crowd of several thousand that welcomed him when he arrived at Waterloo Station. The hymn singing and shouts of "Bless you Billy" filled the station hall. This was an event that I could wholly give myself to. We trained as counsellors, signed up for the choir and loved every minute of it.

The first night of the thirteen-week crusade we sat in the 300 voice choir and watched as the stadium filled to capacity. In many ways I felt myself to be in Billy Graham's shoes as he preached. When it came to the appeal at the close of the address I was on the edge of my seat. "I want you to get up out of your seats and walk to the front," he said. "Jesus went to the cross for you. He now asks you to come and stand at the front and give your life to him." My heart was racing; would anyone respond? The TV cameras were focused on the congregation. The press would have loved to embarrass him. What would they say if no one responded? Please God, I prayed, let it happen; don't let this be a failure, the nation is looking on.

The cowboy Roy Rogers, in full dress, was standing up front to welcome everyone. I thought this is going to put everyone off, for this was London not California. Then in silence as Billy waited, they came, and we experienced what was soon to become a familiar sight of hundreds making their way to the front. Many of those that responded became ministers and would, one day, make the same appeal to the congregations they were to preach to. Those were days of tremendous encouragement which gave me a desire to do the same. Well, not quite the same!! We shall see as the story unfolds.

Haringey was followed by Wembley Stadium and the White City Stadium. These were wonderful days with the tube trains full of people singing, 'This is my Story' and the press changing its mind from saying initially 'Go Home Billy' to 'Well Done, Dr Graham'. Both the Queen and the Prime Minister wanted a personal audience with him.

Halfway through the crusade my call-up papers came for National Service in the Royal Artillery. People have often asked, "Did you enjoy your time in the army?" The answer is a definite "Yes." A fresh challenge, new friends, and the challenge to stand alone as a Christian with men who didn't share my values. I even knelt by my bed to pray every night which was quite a brave thing to do. I can recall counting up to ten and then jumping into bed and waiting for the abuse. However, it never happened. Square bashing, spit and polishing boots, pressing thick khaki uniforms into some sort of shape, workouts in the gym and so on. Laurie, my brother, told me that I would be a number and not a name in the Armed Forces. He was right, I became 23017729 Gunner Powell. My time in the Royal Artillery began with an interesting tour of the UK starting at Oswestry for a scalping haircut and uniform then to Plymouth for square bashing, Bath for further training followed by Carlisle and finally to Ayr in Scotland.

Basic training, or 'boot camp' as the Americans say, started at six in the morning. Kit inspections were a daily routine. Every item of clothing, blankets, boots, etc., had an exact place measured in inches. The highly-polished boots were the result of literally hundreds of hours of 'bull'. On one occasion, on returning to my billet room, I discovered that my bed and the entire contents of my locker were missing. In its place was a brief note saying "Look outside the window 23017729," which I did and saw everything in a muddy heap on the grass. Obviously my efforts were not up to standard.

Late one evening, the Second Lieutenant came into the barrack and said he wanted five volunteers. Needless to say, everyone kept quiet. "Right!" he said. "You five will do," and I was one of the unfortunate five. At least that is what I thought at the time, although since then I have used this story many times when preaching. He marched us down to the gym and told us we were to be the representatives of our billet in a boxing competition which was to take place in a month's time. After many hours of instruction and training, the big night came. Hundreds came to watch the fun. Officers turned out in uniform, even their wives came. It was going to be a fun night for all, except, of course, the anxious boxers. My turn came and facing me in the opposite corner was a monster of a man, bulging muscles, possibly Afro-Caribbean and he didn't smile. He looked really mean and I thought that one swift punch from him would finish this scrap very quickly. Soon we were in the middle of the ring with the referee saying, "Have a clean fight and no holding." I was aware that he was looking worried and he then said something I shall never forget. Looking me straight in the eyes he said, "Don't hit me hard, mate." He must have seen the shocked look on my face. This cannot be true, I thought; he was huge and I knew I didn't stand a chance. So he said it again: "Please don't hit me hard, mate." Who was I to argue? So we played the game. The spectators didn't have much fun out of us. The following bout was even funnier with one of the boxers so terrified of being hurt that he climbed onto the back of his opponent and refused to get off until the fight was cancelled. I think all those watching got their money's worth.

Towards the end of the square bashing days, I had a letter from home telling me that the final service of the Billy Graham crusade was to be broadcast live from Wembley Stadium on the coming Saturday afternoon. Fortunately we had a radio in the barrack room. It had three programmes – the Home, Light and Third. That afternoon I switched on the crusade broadcast and stood with my back to the switch and defied anyone to turn it off. It was music to my ears. Apparently one hundred and twenty thousand people attended, and hundreds made their way to the front when he made the appeal to give their lives over to Jesus Christ.

During my time at Bath I had most weekends free, so I often hitch-hiked home for the weekend. Most servicemen did this and lifts were plentiful. My return journey was by train and paid for by dad. The trains would be packed with National Servicemen. It was always hot, stuffy and smelly. Buses were laid on at the station and we would arrive at camp in the early hours of the morning tired and wanting our beds.

At the Bath camp I did three days CB (confined to barracks). This was for leaving a cobweb under a sink unit in the washroom. I had to report to the Guard Room every three hours in full uniform, then in PT kit an hour later. Lots of 'spud bashing', and forced runs around the camp. Very good discipline, but I don't think I would have said so at the time.

When in Carlisle I attended the Brethren assembly. One of its members was a man called Mr. Carr. He was the owner of Carrs Biscuits of Carlisle. He took pity on the National Servicemen and very kindly invited us back to his mansion for dinner and tea. It was an all-day event and we got on very well. He once kindly invited Ruth up for the weekend. I recall leaving his house late one Sunday evening to catch the bus back to camp. When I boarded the bus I was amused to see a friend of mine wearing my suit and overcoat. He had helped himself to my clothes. I thought it rather funny. He didn't know where to put his face. I was sad to leave the Carrs of Carlisle but the army had other plans and the next posting took me to Scotland followed by demob and back home to Ruth and the family.

I can recall the desperate feeling of not wanting to return to the banking world. I could have done with some help from a Job Centre, but unfortunately they did not exist in those days. So I prayed about it in St Paul's, Ludgate Hill. The Lord must have known my dilemma, for as I walked down the steps of St Paul's I was stopped by a man who I knew through my National Service days in Ayr. I poured out my feelings to him. He replied with some very reassuring words to the effect that God was in control and in time His perfect will would be known to me, and in the meanwhile I should stay in the bank.

I was appointed to the West End Foreign Branch. Once again I found myself wearing a sombre grey suit reporting for 'business' as my father called it. To me it was like a penance – something I had to do. However, the bright side of life was to be with Ruth while saving towards our future.

Ruth's parents now lived in New Zealand and our intentions were to marry and then take a year's trip to N.Z., return home and settle down somewhere. However her father said coming for one year and costing several hundreds of pounds seemed to him to be rather a waste of money and that we should reconsider it. After thinking things through, we decided not to go and the money was spent on brand-new furniture.

We were married at Southfields Baptist Church. Ruth

looked lovely as she came down the aisle. Our vows included, "until death us do part or when Jesus returns." Whatever happens we shall be with Him. It's a real hope. As we came out of the church it started to snow. Ruth's arms were really cold and Laurie, my brother, gave them a good rub to warm them up. The reception was held in a small room in the basement of the church. Our honeymoon was in Teignmouth, Devon. We hired a small Ford Popular car and as usual, friends tied cans on the bumper and we left the church with cheers and waves. Ruth was wearing a pale blue coat and matching felt hat. She was radiant. I could not be happier.

Sadly, Ruth's parents were not at the wedding. Jim, her brother, gave her away. Jenny, my sister and a close friend, Jenny Blaegrove, and eight-year-old Sheila Dare, were the bridesmaids. Madeline and Ray, Laurie and Sheila and all my family, including Grandma Hart, were there to support us. David Bendell, our good friend, was doing his National Service at the time.

We managed to find a top-floor apartment in Laureston Road near Wimbledon Common. As mentioned, we splashed out on new 'G Plan' furniture and had everything we needed. In hindsight I think we should have put a deposit on a house instead. We both continued to work for Barclays Bank. Ruth enjoyed her athletics and netball and I enjoyed watching her. Returning home from work one evening I found Ruth looking pretty pale and shaken. "You won't believe this, Tony, but I fainted at work and I think I am pregnant." Now this was something to take in. She gave me a hug and said, "Don't worry, this is the best thing that could happen to me," and so it was. The pregnancy was painful as she endured early morning sickness, felt the pressure of work and in general was rather exhausted. The final blow came when the landlord said we had to leave the apartment, saying it was unsuitable for children. However, one huge advantage of working in the bank was the offer of a low-interest mortgage for house purchase. This was to be the answer to the problem. Quickly with dad's help we found a very tired house in need of redecoration in Southfields for £1,750 at a time when all the other houses in the road were selling for £3,000 or more. It was in a terrible condition, but it was all we could afford. The day after moving in, Ruth walked with Laurie from our new house to dad's apartment over Barclays Bank, Southfields, where he was the manager. There was a slight hill at the top of the road and she found she could hardly make it. Gasping, she clutched Laurie's arm and said, "I think the baby is coming. I can't go any further." Somehow they managed to reach the bank. From then on it was all action. Dad was used to the journey to Nelson Hospital in Merton. A few days earlier he had taken his other daughter-in-law Sheila to the same hospital for the birth of Andy. Now it was Ruth's turn. People must have wondered what was going on in the local Barclays Bank. Madeline had been there, with her baby Andrea having been born in the same hospital a year previously, followed by Jenny a few years later. Once in hospital the ordeal started. The care was not good and the labour lasted thirty-six hours, but as Ruth often says, you get a prize at the end. What a wonderful prize it was – Christina Ruth Powell arrived – beautiful, fantastic and a total joy to us and all the family. Ruth stayed in hospital for another ten days which gave me time to decorate the kitchen, lounge and bedroom. At least it looked presentable when she returned home with our wonderful 'prize'.

Life was good apart from banking. Much of our time was taken up with mum and dad at the Hope Mission in Merton. It was a tin tabernacle tucked away in the back streets of South Wimbledon. For many years it was home to a handful of people who had done their best to maintain a ministry in the area. It must have been a breath of fresh air for them when dad and mum became pastors. They came with our family in tow plus another dozen or so teenagers from New Malden. It was all-out evangelism with dad leading the way.

We had several week-long missions. Some were inspiring, others less so. The most outrageous preacher was Mrs. Seth Sykes and her amazing magic lantern slides. The show included lightly-clad angels floating over deathbeds, gruesome demons standing at the gates of hell and ragged children standing in dismal streets. The captions at the top of one picture said, 'Are you saved?' and 'Are you ready?' All this in a darkened hall as she played and sang dreary songs in her manly Scottish voice. She also had an unfortunate cough, a sort of nasal snort between each verse, this added to her somewhat unique style. Interesting comments, not all complimentary, came from the young people. My parents thought she was just right for the community in South Wimbledon; they even invited her back for a second mission. I can still see one of the slides with the words 'Knell tolls the Bell' at the bottom and a gruesome picture of a devil ringing a bell and hundreds of ghostly bodies falling down a well.

There was a young family living in the road next to the

mission, Mr. & Mrs. Don Dare, or Don and Doris. They both became Christians during our time there and both their daughter Sheila and their grandchildren have all come to faith. My mother wrote two books about characters in the mission whilst they worshipped there. One book was called 'Spare No Arrows'. One story featured Jimmy Pates. He couldn't read or write, liked a pint and worked as a coalman. He was a great young man full of fun and we got on well together. He had a real relationship with Jesus and everyone knew about it. He later married a woman living opposite 25 Poplar Grove. Their first child was a boy and they called him Tony.

Running the mission was hard work for mum and dad. Three trips every Sunday from New Malden plus several further journeys during the week for various clubs and meetings. Those were the days of Mods and Rockers and also the Teddy Boys. The youth club attracted some of these individuals and one night it all got a little out of hand and finished up with a fight. Fireworks were let off next to mother. This really frightened her and as a result she lost her sense of taste. Sadly she never regained it for the rest of her life.

It must have been a very welcome break for my parents when they decided to spend six months with my older brother Laurie and his wife Sheila who were involved with mission work in the West Amazon. They had an amazing time and came back full of stories. Dad loved to tell of their experiences and often said, "The missionaries tell you what you want to hear; I will tell you the truth." He went into great details about their lack of money, poor diet, the heat, and ferocious insects.

He made me laugh when he told of his experience of fishing on the banks of the Amazon. He took his River Thames tackle to Brazil. Making himself comfortable he cast out into the mighty river. Apparently there was a sudden swirl of water and a huge splash as a monster of a fish made off with his rod and fishing tackle. It nearly took dad with it.

Before moving on from the days at the Hope Mission I have to mention several dedicated elderly folk who were an example to us all. The first that comes to mind was Mr. Densham, who stood about 4'6" high. His thin, weak body and humped back twisted his head to one side. He was a clever man and worked as an accountant in a local firm. He was always very bright and happy every time we met him. My fondest memory of him was during the time we repainted the hall. Not to be left out he got a chair, somehow leaned his twisted body over the chair and painted the lower part of the wall. What a man! One of God's saints.

Then there was 'Chuckles', an elderly man, 5' tall and always dressed in a neatly-pressed blue suit complete with waistcoat, gold chain and watch. He had a large tummy and a beaming red face. After one morning service when he was particularly blessed by the ministry, he stood up and said with his hands resting upon his tummy, "Well everyone, this morning we have had a feast of good things and I want to thank God for it." His prayer was an inspiration to listen to, and he did look contented as he said it.

Then there was Mr. Crouch. He came to know Jesus as his

Friend and Saviour later in life. He had a drink problem which affected his mind. He worked for British Rail in Wimbledon. Dad gave him the job of giving out the weekly notices during the Sunday service. He loved this new responsibility; it gave him a position in the church and of course, helped to rebuild his self-esteem, for everyone supported him. Then came the day when dad asked him to announce the showing of a Billy Graham film called, 'Oil Town USA'. The poor man got very muddled and ended up saying something like this: "Next week there will be a film about Billy Bray living in Oil Town USA. All welcome: no admission." He also got a little confused when he referred publicly to dad. Sometimes he called him, 'Mr. Powell,' other times, 'Mate' and a few times 'Old Cock'. Then he corrected himself and called him, 'Sir.' Every week he managed to get into some sort of a muddle but he always finished by saying, "Well, you know what I mean," and usually we did. We all loved him and so did his Heavenly Father. Back in those days, unlike today, it didn't seem to matter. Everyone needs recognition and a small fellowship is the place for people to develop their gifting. The old Hope Mission certainly gave everyone plenty of opportunity. It was a good place for the young people to learn to preach even if they sometimes made terrible mistakes.

Our journey to the Hope Mission took us along a 40 mph dual carriageway and dad liked to put his foot down on the accelerator. The van's top speed was about 50 mph. Ruth happened to notice on one occasion that we were being followed by a police car and she warned dad. "Great!" was his reply. "We will give him a run for his money," and he promptly went faster. Poor mother hid her head in her hands, saying as she did on many occasion, "Stop it, Doug." The young people in the van loved every minute of this, dad's only reply was "Jehu," whom the Bible says, drove furiously. He managed to reach 50 mph before being pulled over. His lame excuse was, "The young people encouraged me, Officer."

He loved being with young people and children were always captured by his Bible stories. He particularly impressed them when he sang a chorus called 'Only a boy called David' accompanied by great dramatic actions, swinging his arms round and round as David delivered the fatal stone which killed Goliath. He had a very bad bloodshot eye which mother said was caused by his energetic chorus singing. He later had the eye removed and replaced by a glass eye. This gave him an opportunity to amuse his grandchildren when they visited him in his home in Poplar Grove. He played a game with them by removing the eye and putting it though the letter box when they knocked at the door, saying, "I can see you and I'll eat you for breakfast." The children just bounced up and down on their toes with excitement. When the door opened it was all hugs. These were great days for Ruth and the family.

All this time I was still working in the bank but feeling increasingly desperate to get out. I applied to the probation service but was told that I had had too sheltered a background and had no understanding of the criminal world. They were probably right. I felt that the best way of rectifying this was to apply to the Police Force. It was one way to escape from the prison of Barclays Bank. Thankfully, my application was accepted. Within a few weeks I found myself with thirty men sitting exams, medicals and interviews. One of the officers said that he didn't like the way I frowned when answering his questions. I apologised and said my mother had the same problem. Cheek!! I was offered the job which I accepted, although I had no idea what I had let myself into. On leaving the bank I leapt down the front steps, shouting "Freedom at last!" A new chapter was opening up, and furthermore, I would be better paid.

Chapter 2

A Policeman's Lot

I trained at Hendon Police College. It was more demanding than I had anticipated. The course lasted twelve weeks. The lectures covered the law, much of which had to be learned by heart. Mock accidents were set up, first aid, swimming, traffic control and much more. The discipline reminded me of my National Service days. It was a totally different world but I was always in good company. Halfway through the course I was reluctantly allowed three days' leave to be with Ruth when she gave birth to Clifford, our son, at home. This was a stressful time for us. It was a home birth; and she had a difficult time delivering Clifford. Because of various complications he was taken off to Tite Street Hospital for seven days suffering with minor convulsions. Nowadays, of course, no-one would be separated from their newborn baby. Thank God, he soon recovered and suffered no ill effects from the trauma. However, Tina, our daughter, aged two and a half rose to the occasion and did her best to care for Ruth. She was amazing, and of course my mum and dad were just around the corner to help. Now we had two very special little people to care for.

Soon my training was completed and I found myself stationed at Putney Police Station. I was accompanied

around 'The Manor' by an officer in his forties. My first
tour of duty was at night time. We walked the beat for a
couple of hours until my colleague needed a rest; he soon
found a convenient park bench and chatted away about
'the Job' as it was called by the men. He finished the
conversation by saying, "Don't forget, young man, you
are not paid for what you do, but for what you might have
to do." He then went to sleep. Wow, I thought, I'm getting
paid for this. An hour later we left the park. Not quite the
drama of programmes about the police on TV.

Some months later I was walking down Putney High
Street just after midnight. A man stopped me and said he
had seen someone hiding behind a sofa in the furniture
shop. I went back to the shop with him but I couldn't
see anyone. However, he insisted he had, so I called the
station for backup. The patrol car arrived with the duty
inspector, sergeant and several police with a dog to search
the premises. We all had to wait till the keyholder arrived.
This took a long time as he had a journey of several miles.
This was so frustrating. As far as I was concerned, if
anyone had been in the building they presumably would
have seen or heard the police outside the shop and would
have escaped already. I decided to search the back of
the premises, taking a colleague with me; however, we
couldn't see any forced entry. I then suggested that we
should check the flat roof over the shops. This meant
climbing a drain pipe. He refused to come with me, saying
with a laugh, "You are on your own, mate." "Thanks a lot,"
I thought. It was really dark on the roof and difficult to
see the glass panels, wires and cables. It was a dangerous
place at night time. No wonder he didn't want to come
with me. I didn't expect to find anyone. Then the action

started. Two men leapt at me. They had been hiding behind a chimney stack. More out of shock than bravery I grabbed hold of the nearest one and somehow whipped his arm up his back. To my amazement he collapsed at my feet. The other said, "You ain't got me, mate," and ran. Desperate for help and alone I shouted, "Check the back, he is doing a runner." I pulled out my whistle and blew with all my might, but nothing happened, as the whistle was full of fluff. I had never blown the thing since I put it in my pocket two years ago. The 'runner' leapt off the roof, landed in a nearby garden and was never seen again. My pathetic youngster stumbled across the roof and slid down the drainpipe where my colleague was waiting for him. Once in the van he burst into tears saying he had met the other man in a local pub and had never done anything like this before. A likely story! When the keyholder did eventually arrive, we found they had packed the safe with explosives and if it had blown up it would have taken the shop with it. Perhaps we saved their lives – who knows. My youngster spent the next six months in prison. I don't know what happened to his mate. It was one of the best night duties I ever had – real police work.

I once talked of that event at a ladies' meeting. I could see that an elderly lady sitting in the front row was really living the story with me. In a hushed voice to add to the drama, I said, "I crept across the roof looking for villains." I then paused and looked across the congregation as if looking for the villain and then raising my voice, I shouted, "Got you." The elderly lady was so engrossed that she cried out, "Oh." At the same time her false teeth shot out and finished up at my feet. Ruth just covered her face. The children giggled away. I knew Ruth could not bring herself to pick the teeth up, so it was left to me. It was a meeting never to be forgotten. The moral of the story was "Pray regularly, in other words blow your whistle – keep open to God." Don't let fluff i.e. wrong attitudes – build up in your life. You will then be able to meet any emergency. However that evening will be remembered for the teeth rather than my talk.

About that time, the CND attracted a lot of the public's attention and demonstrations were commonplace. There was to be a huge one in Trafalgar Square. Several hundred police officers were drafted in including me. The time came when we were ordered to clear the Square and to take seven prisoners each. All mine co-operated and were no trouble, that is, except one. I had to drag him across the Square then into the coach, and somehow get him into a seat. At the police station the troubles really began. The following morning I was in court with three of my prisoners. All pleaded guilty till the 'awkward one' said, "Not guilty." He then accused me of kicking him in his privates, dragging him across the Square, bruising his shins on the coach steps and soaking him with a hose in the police yard, before finally beating him up in the cells. I can still hear the roars of encouragement coming from his mates at the back of the court. The magistrate turned to me and said, "What have you to say in response to this?" In all honesty all I could say was, "I did not witness any violence against this man." However, I did know that prior to him being charged I was approached by two officers who said, "If you are having trouble with this man we will deal with him." I was not aware that they had beaten him up in the cells. However, from that time on he was no trouble to me. Previously he had to be dragged everywhere. This all took place at 2am. He was found guilty and that was the end of it, at least so I thought. Unknown to me I had arrested a relation of R.A. Butler, the current Home Secretary. The following week there appeared a full-page article in the New Statesman magazine quoting my police number as the arresting officer. I was accused of everything in the book. Needless to say, Scotland Yard wanted to interview me and soon I was being interrogated for hours by senior officers. The burning issue was who had beaten him up in the cells. I had no idea. At two in the morning with literally hundreds of police crammed into police stations charging hundreds if not thousands of protestors, it was mayhem and I had no idea who these officers were. Of course as the arresting officer I was responsible for my prisoner and should not have let him out of my sight. Before I left Scotland Yard I produced a ten-page statement covering this unfortunate event. I went home a very worried man, in need of some good advice. My uncle Frank Powell, who was a Metropolitan Magistrate, said he would give me a reference if things got nasty for me. I could have lost my job. Thank God that never happened, and I never heard anything further about the incident.

Late turn was from two in the afternoon till ten. The sun was shining as I walked along Putney embankment one day. In the distance I could see a man trying to break into several cars. As I got nearer to him he managed to open a door and get in. He had no idea that I was a few yards away. His look of amazement was something else when I opened the door and said, "So what's going on, mate?" and his inspired reply was, "I'm looking for the time, officer," to which I replied, "Well, mate, you could always ask a policeman." It was an easy arrest and as I walked him down to the police box on Putney Bridge, he pleaded with great emotion saying, "Go on, mate, let me off, I promise never to do it again." I was almost tempted to let him go but seeing I was still on probation I needed a few arrests to justify my ability as a PC.

Early morning shift put me on the street at six in the morning. I had a bit of fun looking out for my sister Jennifer and her husband Brian, who would drive into Putney to go to work. I would watch out for their car coming down the hill into Putney and then step out into the road and flag them down. Of course they had to stop. It was a lot of fun on my part but not for them if they were late for work. This was one of those stories which when we are together now, we say, "Do you remember?"

After two years' probation I was fully qualified and transferred to Scotland Yard where I joined the 'A' department. I worked alongside a Chief Superintendent and a Sergeant looking after the administration of the mounted branch. I remember the sergeant nearly exploding when he saw me attempting to type. "What the **** have we got here? Can you type?" With a bit of cheek I said, "It's okay Sarge. In a week or two I will be as good as you." I don't think I ever was. Nevertheless, I was in that office for another two or three years. It was an easy life; the hours were good and I had every weekend off. A young police cadet by the name of David Austin was attached to my office for work experience. Some time later he told me that I shared my faith with him. Little did I know that in years to come we would become great friends. Later, when I was based in Battersea, I met him on the doorsteps of the church in Austin Road, by which time he had risen to the rank of Inspector.

My office was located above the stables in Great Scotland Yard, so I had frequent opportunities to chat to the officers in the mounted branch. One of the men was the proud rider of the horse used by the Queen for Trooping the Colour. One day, he asked me, "Do you know why this old fella never disgraces himself when ridden by the Queen?" I had no idea. His answer was, "It's simple – I don't give him anything to drink for two days before any ceremonial event." No wonder the poor old horse always had its head down when on parade.

During this time we moved from Pirbright Road in Southfields to Ely Close in New Malden. It was a mock-Tudor house close to the Coombe golf course. I think we were a little proud to be living in such a good location. It was here that Richard was born. That was a great day. The birth took place at Kingston Hospital. I was allowed in after the birth, dressed in a green robe and wearing a face mask. Ruth says she recognised my eyes. This time the birth was free from complications. Now we had three children and they were a great joy to us. Ruth still thinks back to the days of skipping along the lane, pushing the pram and singing silly songs. She was a very happy mum. Most mornings she would go round to my parents and join them for a late breakfast. Dad used to give the children his 'tit bits' from his breakfast plate. The children, although well fed, always looked for more from their granddad at breakfast time. The home at 25 Poplar Grove holds so many happy memories for all my family.

In my late twenties I continued to feel the call to a Christian ministry. I clearly recall being very impressed as a young child at 'The Hall' by a London City missionary telling stories of his work amongst the marginalised of London. I said to myself that this was the work I would do one day.

Ruth and mum got on very well together. One day they attended a meeting where a lady was speaking about the Royal National Mission to Deep Sea Fishermen. On her return home Ruth was full of enthusiasm and felt this would be just right for me. So the next move was initially down to Ruth, which was a good thing, as within two months we had sold our beautiful home and said goodbye to church friends. Soon we were on our way to the Fishermen's Mission in Lowestoft in my parents' car. During the course of the journey we began singing, 'I have decided to follow Jesus, no turning back, no turning back'. Mum's quick comment was, "Just as well, you two: it's a bit late to turn back now."

It really was a dramatic change in lifestyle, and one that we shall never regret. It just opened up a new way of life far removed from London suburbia, and of course the 'seaside' still had a magic pull for all the family.

Chapter 3

Fishermen's Mission

My time with the Mission took us from Lowestoft to Grimsby, then from Grimsby to Scrabster, then to Lerwick, on to Ayr and then to our final posting to Fraserburgh, quite some journey with three children. I don't think the boys worried too much about the constant moving but we know Tina found it very stressful as she often left behind her favourite friends. We felt so sorry about this and in recent years we have talked it through which I believe has helped us all. The problem was that I signed an agreement stipulating that I would move according to the decisions of the Mission Council. Most men in the mission moved as frequently as we did and we were no exception to the rule.

What can I say about Lowestoft and the subsequent missions? I will just have to pick out the special events from the daily routine. Lowestoft was a very busy mission. Bill Newell was the Superintendent and I was one of his three assistants. We all wore a naval uniform. The mission was on the dockside, with thirty bedrooms, a busy canteen, lounge with television, chapel and a sick bay. As in all missions, we also had domestic staff for cooking and cleaning.

Into this building came fishermen with big pay packets

in their pockets, after several weeks of fishing in the Icelandic waters. Many of the men staying with us were from broken families, some were running away from the police, many had served prison sentences, and more than a few had drink problems. So mix that all together and quite an explosive situation could develop when after wine, women and song, they returned to the mission and their bedrooms.

It wasn't unusual for men with a few drinks inside them to want to go into the chapel and pray. Bearing in mind the risk of their throwing up all over the chapel floor, we guided them to their bedrooms with the promise that they could pray in the morning when sober, which never happened.

I have often said that I met more villains in the mission than I ever did in the police. Just a couple of events prove the point. It was 11pm on a cold winter's night. Most of the men were in their rooms, while a few were watching television. The doorbell rang and on opening the door I beheld a drunk fisherman. In a slurred voice he said, "Any beds left?" The truth was that we were full, so I simply said "Sorry, we are full." I had hardly got the word 'Full' out when his huge fist delivered a blow on my nose. I found myself flat on my back wondering how he managed that when drunk. He disappeared down the road and I made my way to the toilet to wash my bloody nose. Thanks a lot, mate, do come again!

A similar incident happened when someone pulled a knife on me after I told him we were full. This time I ran and he chased me around the building. The police were called and he spent the night in another bedroom called a 'cell'. One of the long-remembered characters of Lowestoft was a huge man called Mad Murdoch. He had a gravel-like voice and was a very violent man. He loved to show you the scars in the palms of his hands. Knowing the staff were Christians, he liked to play on this and breathing heavy alcoholic fumes into our faces he would say, "These are the hands of Jesus." He often came into the mission for his meals, although if he was drunk he would not be allowed in. On one such occasion he got a little upset to say the least. So in order to show that he would not be told what he should or should not do, he picked up a huge piece of concrete, staggered across the road, just missing all the busy traffic, and hurled the concrete through the huge plate-glass window. Several men were asleep in the lounge chairs recovering from drinking sessions. They were covered with glass splinters. It was total mayhem as Mad Murdoch staggered into the lounge. A fight was about to break out. Bill Newell called the police. To add to the drama, one of the men in the lounge said to the officer, "Charge Murdoch with assault, the glass has cut my head." The officer suddenly recognised this man from a previous incident and arrested him along with Mad Murdoch.

The late turn from four in the afternoon till midnight was always a scary time. The simple task of turning off the TV at 11.30 pm in the lounge could be a daunting experience. With twenty men watching a programme that finished at midnight and others wanting a different channel and some just being plain awkward, it was no easy task. Also, by then I was tired and wanted my bed. So it was into the lions' den with a firm voice to wake the sleepers and impress the sober, saying, "Okay gentlemen, it's time for bed," and off went the television. I will not print the responses.

There was only one man who really worried me, an individual by the name of Barry Gordon. He was about twenty-five years of age with a shock of ginger hair and plenty of tattoos. He was a very violent young man, with a long police record. He loved a fight when he was drunk, although when sober he was quite peaceful. He knew I was in the police once and would taunt me saying I could never pin him down with an armhold called the 'hammer lock and bar'. One day the opportunity arose and to my own amazement I whipped his arm up his back and his other arm around his neck. He was powerless and also very impressed. I was even more impressed as I had never used this arrest in the police. He never forgot this and developed a deep respect for me even when he was drunk and refused a bed. A new Superintendent joined the staff and I warned him about Barry, saying if he was drunk to refuse him a bed. He chose to ignore this advice and the following evening he was badly beaten up by Barry. He ripped the lapels off his jacket, tore his shirt open and sank his fang-like teeth into his chest ripping open the skin. This was his favourite way of fighting. He would remove his upper four front false teeth and use his two canine teeth to tear into his victim. It really was no holds barred with him and I am thankful for my experiences of life, army and the police service.

Some of our time was also spent in visiting retired fishermen and widows, meeting the men on the boats and whenever the occasion was right, sharing our faith with the men. We had many opportunities to do this. On Sundays we gave the domestic staff a day off, while the uniformed staff provided a free afternoon tea for the residents. This was usually a salad with cold tongue and ham, with plenty of tea. We cleaned up the tables, washed up and swept the floor while the men went into the lounge, most of them to sleep. About this time a few local Christians would come in to attend the afternoon service. This was held in the lounge with most of the men fast asleep. So very quietly a few chairs were put behind them and hymn books were placed on their laps. The opening song was announced and the captive audience woke thinking they were in heaven – at least that is what they later said. The short talk seemed to be well received and I believe they enjoyed the hymn singing. We never had any complaints and after all, they had had a free tea.

One Sunday we invited Bernard Clampton, the Superintendent, to tea and just before he arrived my son Richard fired his new toy cannon down the passage way and sent the ball through the front door window. Bernard has never forgotten this. On another occasion Richard climbed the ladders to the rooftop. Our next door neighbour was white with fright thinking he would fall any moment. I climbed the ladder and he was safely brought down. The comment from the next door neighbour was, "He's a bright lad, that one."

Each year the mission staff were involved in an anniversary service at the Fishermen's Bethel not far from the mission. During our year in Lowestoft we sat with local dignitaries on the platform. The programme said that the mayor was to give the Bible reading. The preacher unfortunately had left his sermon notes on the reading desk next to the Bible, and when the mayor stood to read the Bible he picked up the sermon notes by mistake and started to read the sermon. The poor preacher's mouth dropped open, while the chairman was in total shock. "You've got to stop him," gasped the preacher as he heard his sermon read by the mayor. By this time the mayor was in full flow and seemed to be enjoying the opportunity. I seem to remember there was a lot of coughing as the chairman picked up the Bible, handed it to the mayor and made some excuse to cover everyone's embarrassment. You can imagine the embarrassment afterwards, I don't think the mayor knew what was going on, and it didn't seem to bother him. Maybe he was a little worse for drink – who knows.

Ruth was involved in the fishermen's wives' weekly meeting in the chapel. This group of ladies did a wonderful job in supporting the mission with 'Sales of Work' and other fundraising events. At one meeting, they sang the hymn 'Anywhere with Jesus I will gladly go'. Ruth whispered to her friend next to her, "Anywhere but Grimsby." Within a few days we received a letter from the London HQ telling us to pack our bags and prepare to move to Grimsby.

Chapter 4

Grimsby

Grimsby dock area is a grim and grimy place, so no wonder Ruth had said, "Anywhere but Grimsby." The mission, built with granite stone, solid and uninviting, was directly opposite the main gates leading into the fish market and dock area. Inside the building it was drab, tired, and smelt of cooking. The canteen was filled daily with dock workers and fishermen, with not a woman in sight. This was a working man's domain and woe betide any woman who dared to enter. I don't think Ruth or the children ever visited the building.

The mission had forty bedrooms and these were full every night. Don Tucker was the Superintendent. Standing 6'5", an ex-sailor, he was more than able to deal with the unruly characters who used the mission – and there were plenty of these. I seem to be giving a pretty depressing picture but it was depressing – an awful old Victorian building that needed to be knocked down. The men had no respect for it and the staff didn't like working there. The Mission Council decided to demolish it, and within two years we were in a brand new building full of light, colour and everything to be proud of.

What a contrast to the old one! The fishermen's attitude

changed towards both the staff and the building. It had superb facilities – a games room, library, two canteens, laundry, sixty bedrooms, and a beautiful chapel, with four apartments for the uniformed staff. The domestic staff increased to a dozen or so. Sir William Duthie, chairman of the mission, presided over the opening ceremony on a specially constructed stage outside the main entrance. The mayor, councillors, local ministers and invited guests filled the stage. Several hundred were present and heard Sir William say that the new mission was, "The finest of its kind in all the world." Although I suppose you could say that about anything, never mind – it was a great day.

The day's celebration included an evening concert held in the chapel, with the showing of the new mission publicity film called 'Men Apart'. It was my task to operate the film projector. Sir William Duthie introduced the film. It was obvious from his remarks that he was very proud of it. Everyone settled back to enjoy the show. The lights were dimmed and I started the film. So far so good, until I realised that the take-up spool was not receiving the used film, in fact it was spilling onto the floor. Groans were coming from the people sitting nearby who could see what was happening. With a few thousand feet still to come I could see we would soon be knee deep in film. Soon people would be trampling on it. This film was Sir William's pride and joy and he looked forward to it being shown all over the country, raising funds for the mission and boosting its profile. I had no option but to stop the film and say, "Sorry, ladies and gentlemen. There has been a slight technical problem. It will soon be resolved." I flipped a couple of switches and hoped for the best. Lights went down again and I started the film from the beginning.

To my horror the film again refused to be taken up by the offending spool. More groans of sympathy from those sitting nearby. Sir William knew nothing of this. He was sitting in the front row with the mayor. It was then that George came to the rescue with a huge cardboard box. Thirty minutes later the credits came up on the screen and before the lights came on, George had made a very quick exit with the box. The congregation clapped, Sir William beamed and Don Tucker, who probably knew what was going on, was proud of his staff.

Both Tina and Clifford, our children, were in the local junior school and it wasn't long before Richard, our youngest son, joined them. We met them at the school gates as did most parents. However, not long after Richard had joined the school, he decided he didn't need our company. He managed to slip out of the playground, intent on making his way home. He didn't make it. The school staff were embarrassed, police were informed and I went on a frantic search. The back streets of Grimsby were not the best place for a child to roam around on his own. Back at school Ruth was relieved to hear the police say he had been found and in very good shape. Within a short while we collected our son – totally unfazed by all the fuss. The officer said, "He's a bright lad this one. Don't smack him, mum: he knew his address and where he was going." True, this was not bad for a boy who had only been in Grimsby for a few days, but he didn't do it again. Maybe his pocket money was affected. I can't remember.

An important part of the mission's ministry was the weekly visit to the local prison. This was the responsibility of the Superintendent and on this occasion he asked me to accompany him. I jumped at the opportunity. The chapel was packed and we joined the procession of local clergy, the prison governor and others to reserved seats in the front row. As we walked down the aisle several fishermen who knew us called out to him saying, "Keep a bed for me, Super," "See you next week" or "Get me a berth." The clergy ignored the banter apart from Don. The governor was not impressed.

The mission really placed us in the front line of the industry. These were rough, tough men working in rusty old trawlers sailing the Icelandic waters under terrible conditions. If the weather was bad they would have some stories to tell us on their return. As the weeks went by, we really had some good times sharing their experiences. Not all were drunkards. Although we didn't see any making a profession of faith, we hoped they understood we wanted to be their friends.

We had a strict no alcohol policy on the mission premises. This, as is obvious from the previous chapter, was a necessity. One day when in the old building, I was in the canteen around lunchtime. One of the many well-known characters was walking across the canteen with a full dinner plate in one hand and a cup of tea in the other plus two very large bottles of cheap VP wine sticking out of his pockets. He had often been refused a bed in the mission because of his heavy drinking. "Sorry," I said, "you know, Jock, you are not allowed drink in the mission." He was not amused as I said it in front of his mates. They were all quite merry. "So," he said, "who is going to stop me?" "Okay," I said, "I am." With that, he let go of his dinner plate and cup of tea. The smash of the plate and cup attracted everyone's attention. His fists came up, and putting his face inches from mine he said, "Right, take me on, mission man." His breath stank of alcohol. "No problem," I said. "Not here but outside." I couldn't believe what I was saying. He staggered towards the door while the rest of the canteen must have wondered who would win the punch-up. The sight of a mission man fighting in the street with a fisherman wasn't quite the image one would expect. However, getting to the door leading to the street I opened it, gave him a mighty shove and slammed the door with me safely in the building. So far so good. I returned to the canteen to the cheers of the men who were following the events with huge interest. Then suddenly, there was a loud crash and glass was flying everywhere. The two full bottles of VP wine were splattered on the stone floor of the canteen. Outside the building my drunken friend was dancing about waving his arms feeling he had won the battle after all. But who really had won the day? A good question. He sobered up in a prison cell and I retired to the office wondering if I could have handled it a little better. I can't remember what the Superintendent thought about it all. Within days he was back on a trawler and no doubt soon forgot about it. I don't remember seeing him again.

Ruth and I developed a real friendship with Don Tucker and his wife and we had plans to work together on a number of projects. The new building opened up many new opportunities but the Mission Council had other ideas and they said that Scrabster in the North of Scotland was to be our next port of call.

We were so excited, I had previously been on an Assistant Superintendents' conference in Dumfries and just loved

Scotland, so I longed to work there. It was all too good to be true. It was promotion and although quite a small mission, I would be the boss. We bade our sad farewells at Grimsby Station and were soon on a steam train heading north. Within hours we were travelling through magnificent mountain scenery near Inverness. None of us had been that far before and we were loving every minute. We even had a three-course dinner in the dining carriage – something we could never have afforded before. All this at the mission's expense. Seeing they were only paying me £700 a year I think they could afford to bless us with a little luxury. The steam train added to the excitement of the journey. When the children put their faces out of the window they soon discovered their faces rapidly became covered in black smuts.

Chapter 5

Scrabster

The Scrabster mission was right on the harbour wall and we lived above it in a three-bedroom apartment. The fishermen were local family men and they warmly welcomed us. The canteen, unlike Grimsby, offered no threats to women and children. It was well used by everyone in the community. The staff could not have been nicer and during our entire time there we never saw a single drunk fisherman.

The fishing port nestled beneath the hills. The small harbour gave shelter to thirty small fishing boats and a few yachts. The fish market was supplied with the local daily catch. Ruth and the family loved the freedom to use the mission and the dock area without any physical threat or embarrassment. She soon found she had a task to do in baking a hundred sausage rolls every day for hungry fish merchants and dock workers who used the small refreshment hut not far from the mission. She also had responsibility for the small ladies' meeting. I looked after the Sunday evening service in the mission. For us it was the beginning of a new phase in our ministry. The buck stopped with us. We enjoyed the challenge and responsibility. Week after week we applied what little we knew of God's heart towards the thirty or so local folk, and were made very welcome by them. I invited the local school choir to sing at our first mission anniversary service. They were brilliant and, of course, the building on this occasion was packed with admiring parents. They sang three pieces and one was in Gaelic. After the Gaelic piece, I asked what it was about and the reply was not what I was expecting. The teacher said, with a sort of apology, "It was a song to a lovesick cow."

In every mission we had an advisory committee made up of local people. In Scrabster this was chaired by Mr. John Sinclair, the Lord Lieutenant for the county. He was also the welcome sergeant at the Salvation Army. What a man! He stood 6'6" high and everyone knew him. He chaired our welcome service. Among other things he said with a wry smile, "We will either love you or hate you." I can't recall my reply. The whole atmosphere was so different from our previous mission. It was a small community, friendly and welcoming.

My mum and dad visited us. Mum loved Scotland. She used to play an old 'seventy eight' record called 'Going through the flood'. It was about a doctor visiting a patient on a stormy night, sung in a strong Scottish accent. So she was pleased to be with real Scottish people. Unfortunately she found it hard to understand what they were saying at times. On one occasion she agreed to have tea with an elderly lady and returned without knowing what she had said.

On Sunday we took them to the local Church of Scotland morning service. I knew that one man in the congregation always sang bass at the top of his voice, and could easily be heard above everyone else. Dad also loved to sing tenor at full volume. So with a little bit of manoeuvring I managed to sit dad next to him. He knew nothing about my plan. At the first hymn they both burst into song. Their voices blended in worship and the volume increased. Everyone could hear them. Afterwards dad said with a knowing look, "Tony, thanks for the interesting seating arrangement." I knew that dad just loved to sing about the Lord and what better way than in the company of a kindred spirit. I believe the tenor and the bass had a good chat afterwards. The children thought it was hilarious and so did a few others in the congregation.

Our children had to face another school and find new friends. This is always the downside of mission life. At the end of one term they came home with the usual school reports. On the bottom of one report it said, "This child talks too much." On the reverse side there was a section asking for comments from parents. I could not resist writing, "You should meet his mother." Ruth now tells me I am making this up and suffering from a senior moment, but I don't think so. The children were free to ride their bikes around the harbour area. Unfortunately Clifford got a little too close to the edge and tumbled twenty feet onto a pile of ropes on the boat deck. Several fishermen came to the rescue saying, "Don't move, son, stay calm. It's going to be all right; the ambulance is coming." The crew lifted him off the deck in a straitjacket and took him to Wick hospital. After examination he was pronounced fit and well. I think Cliff quite enjoyed the attention and the experience didn't put him off cycling around the harbour.

The Castle of Mey was the country home of the Queen

Mother. Every year The Royal Yacht Britannia called at the harbour when she was in residence and John Sinclair would be present in his amazing uniform to meet her when she stepped ashore. Often the royal children would be on board and they could be heard calling out, "Hallo Granny!" as their boat drew alongside the harbour wall. During her summer stay at the castle she would often visit the shops in the village. The story goes that on one occasion when in the village she was overheard saying to her lady-in-waiting that she was intending to call on John Sinclair on her return trip to the castle. Someone overheard this and dashed round to John's house with the news. He was out at the time. When the Queen Mother arrived, John's sister answered the door in her dressing gown and curlers. That story went around the village for years. John didn't deny it. We met socially on several occasions during our all too short stay in Scrabster. He even let me try on his Lord Lieutenant's uniform. I should have taken a photograph.

The big event and headache of the year was the annual Carnival and Sale of Work. This was the first time I had the overall responsibility for organising such an event. The advisory committee worked very hard with me to ensure its success. Through various contacts we arranged a fly-past of Buccaneer aircraft, a piano-smashing competition, a salmon on the end of a greasy pole and an underwater frogman event. Then, of course, there were the usual tables filled with cakes and knitting. Over a thousand people came – filling the harbour area outside the mission. Captain Marrack, a submariner who lived locally, opened the event by commending the work of the mission and highlighting the need for financial support. Tina, our daughter, looking absolutely gorgeous, walked across the large platform and presented his wife with a bouquet of flowers. This was followed by John Sinclair making a short speech saying, "Caithness's main industry was coffee mornings and sales of work." The crowd loved that remark but of course it was a joke. The fishing industry, farming and the atomic power station a few miles up the road were all vital parts of the local economy.

The event started with twenty lads in bathing trunks attempting to negotiate the 30' greasy pole that stretched out over the harbour wall and grab the salmon tied to the end. Hundreds were watching and to my horror the first one along the pole took it without any effort. Some quick thinking was needed and I negotiated with him an appropriate price. He replaced the salmon, more grease was applied to the pole and the fun resumed. Meanwhile the Boys' Brigade and Scouts were smashing up pianos and passing each piece through a rubber tyre. Not everyone was comfortable with this bit of fun, but the pianos were old bangers. The fly-past was a complete waste of time as the cloud ceiling was low and all we heard was the roar as they passed overhead. Everyone waved frantically but they didn't return. The biggest disappointment was the supposed display by the local aquatic club. They dived in and we never saw them again. They were supposed to release balloons tied to the bottom of the harbour. All we could see was a trail of bubbles. Not the best entertainment of the afternoon, but you can't win them all. At the end of the day, we raised over a thousand pounds.

Just a few hundred yards from the mission was the lighthouse and Tina in particular became a special friend of one of the children who lived there. We enjoyed family walks along the cliff tops and the opportunities to go fishing. Once a dead cow was washed up on the shore. We all remember the time when six kittens were born in the children's bedroom cupboard. We kept a beautiful ginger one and the rest just disappeared – at least that's what the children were told.

I also had the responsibility of two other missions – one in Kirkwall on the Orkney Isles and the other at Kinlochbervie. It was quite an adventure to visit them. One required a ferry trip and the other a hundred-mile drive along narrow roads to the west coast just beneath Cape Wrath. What a privilege, and what a contrast from the dusty pavements of Putney and the police. I did this trip to Kinlochbervie several times and on one occasion during the winter months we only passed three cars during the entire journey.

Chapter 6

Lerwick

Once again the mission council decided to move us on and so a short plane trip took us to Lerwick in the Shetland Islands. It was situated on a hill with a grass slope in front, newly built, with twenty bedrooms, large canteen, library, TV room, two snooker tables and showers. We were welcomed by Jim Ralph and his wife Eileen, the Assistant Superintendent and his wife. They became lifelong friends. He in turn introduced us to the staff and then to our apartment at the top of the building. The view was outstanding. The entire harbour could be seen below, while across the water we could see the island of Bressay. The fishing fleet was much larger than Scrabster. Boats were often present from Norway, Iceland, and Spain; huge Russian whaling boats visited, their decks covered with whale meat. Peterhead and Fraserburgh boats were regular visitors. It really was great to be in the canteen and hear the different languages. The snooker tables and showers were always in demand.

We soon settled into the routine and enjoyed working with the willing staff who made such a difference to our lives and the running of the mission. This included a small group of ladies that met every week to 'knit for the mission'. What amazing skills they had! These Shetland knitting patterns had been passed on from generation to generation. They knitted complicated patterns and chatted at the same time. A leather pouch strapped around their waist held one needle and the other was held in the right hand and seemed to move faster than the eye could see. Ruth's conventional style and somewhat slower pace were the butt of a lot of jokes. These were ladies born on the island and they often spoke of the hard times in the crofts and fishing industry.

Maggie lived in a large granite house in one of the steep lanes leading off the main high street. The front door took you into a huge kitchen complete with a peat burning stove. She loved to entertain and everything she said was accompanied by a chuckle. With a smile on her weather-beaten face she would say, "Come you in, sit you down and have a cup of tea." I just wish I could hear the Shetland accent again. She was in her late seventies and could tell stories of Shetland life in the crofts when a living was scraped together from farming, knitting and fishing. They were hard times but she and her husband survived all the hardships. We enjoyed many cups of tea with her and the family. Weather was often the topic of conversation. She called a force-eight gale a 'Moorie-Caavie'. If one of these was expected, the parents were called to the school to collect the children in case they were blown over by the heavy gusts of wind.

The children were the right age for another addition to the family, this time in the shape of a beautiful golden Labrador puppy. He was a stunning dog with a finely-shaped head. We named him 'Thor'. He took a strong liking to Ruth and as a puppy would only sleep under her side of the bed. If I took him on a short walk and took the lead off he would immediately make a dash for home and Ruth. We regularly passed a huge Saint Bernard dog on our frequent walks to the 'Knab'. For some reason nearly every time we passed by he would relieve himself and a flood of urine would pour endlessly from his huge body. This amused and amazed the boys, although I'm not sure how Tina reacted. The prospect of meeting this dog certainly encouraged them out of the house when they would rather be watching the telly.

Our trips to the beaches around the island were fun and we even managed the occasional swim in the icy waters. Ruth remembers how after a thirty-second dip she decided to run along the beach at speed to warm up her numbed body. When she sat down, she discovered her foot was pouring with blood, apparently cut on a piece of glass, but her foot was too numb to feel it when running along the beach.

Needless to say the mission had its quota of characters that used the building. Willum was one of them. He was short, heavily built, red faced, and had an unusual stutter. He would never look directly at you. He also suffered from particularly pungent BO. I don't think he ever washed his clothes or his body. He needed a lot of support, understanding and love in his life. As friendship developed we managed to get him to agree to shower. This also gave us an opportunity to set him up with new clothes. Surprisingly, in view of his circumstances, he did in fact have a reasonable singing voice. He had been asked to sing at the local Pentecostal church and before his solo he introduced himself by saying, "I am going to sing, 'All the way to Calvary he went for me', and the Pastor is going to follow me on the organ." He later told me, "Everyone burst out laughing, Mr. Powell, and I don't know why. What did I do wrong?" I could understand the laughter but how could I tell him?

We tried to look after him. On one occasion he sat in front of us in church and the smell was so overpowering that Ruth placed several scent-impregnated pads on the pew ledge behind him. Tina remembers this very well as one of the pads went 'splat' on the floor. Ruth suppressed her laughter and the children held their noses. Ruth tells me I wasn't with them at the time as apparently I was at the front taking the service. I obviously missed all the fun in the pews.

Our television lounge was packed with every nationality when we watched the first man walk on the moon. What an amazing day that was! We also did a good trade in the canteen. One Christian fisherman from Peterhead stopped me on the steps of the mission and said that God would never allow a man to walk on the moon. However, God didn't intervene, and I have often wondered how my friend came to reconcile this with his belief. We all have to work out our faith in a changing world; it's not an easy ride for many of us. I recall one preacher saying that doubt was a God-given gift so that we could come to the knowledge of the truth. Faith would not be required if we didn't suffer from doubt. Without faith it is impossible to please God. However, the rewards are great.

Sick and injured fishermen were frequently landed at the dockside and on many occasions I took them to the hospital. Simple injuries were treated in the mission. One tall heavily-built Russian only needed a small injection.

At the sight of the needle he fainted. The poor man was obviously terrified of needles. He flopped across my desk and scattered papers everywhere. "Great," said the doctor and gave him the injection before he recovered.

We soon built up a very good relationship with several friendly Christian fishermen from Peterhead. George Duncan and his sons were our favourites. Their boat was called 'Fragrance'. They always attended the Sunday Nightcap and made such a difference as they loved to sing the well-known gospel songs. One Sunday, they invited the family to the boat for tea. This included a huge helping of red jelly made in their washing-up bowl. Ruth has never forgotten this, but I seem to remember she had a jolly good helping. Every time they came ashore they gave us a 'fry'. They often fished for herring and used the old drift net routine. They referred to the herring catch as 'silver darlings'. They were a great family. George was also on the advisory council at Peterhead Deep Sea Mission. It was a terrible shock to us and the entire fishing community when we heard he had been washed overboard and drowned. His death was such an overwhelming loss to everyone, especially his family. The funeral service packed the Peterhead Baptist Church. Everyone in Peterhead knew George and the family.

Christmas was soon upon us and we learned that Father Christmas had never put in an appearance in any of the stores or public halls. Here was an opportunity to put the mission further on the map and make a few pennies. I got busy and turned the end of the main hall into a Christmas Grotto. One of the staff agreed to be Father Christmas. We bought about fifty or so small presents for the children.

However, word had got round and eager parents brought their children along in droves. The fifty presents soon disappeared and the queue stretched down the road. Hence a hasty dash to the local stores for more presents. Twenty years later when my son, Clifford, worked for the mission in Peterhead, he was approached by a fisherman who said, "Was your father in Lerwick?" "Yes," he replied. "Well," he said, "I have a bone to pick with him. As a boy I once queued up for thirty minutes to see Father Christmas and all I got was a plastic toy car." "You're lucky," said Cliff. "All I got was -------!" They had a good laugh and shared lots of memories.

One of the outstanding events during our time in Shetland was the visit of the Queen and Royal Family on board The Royal Yacht Britannia. Ruth and I received an invitation from Buckingham Palace to be part of the celebration. It was the 500th anniversary of Norway handing over the Shetland Isles to the UK. The big day came, and we reported to the Lerwick harbour office to be taken by a small launch to Britannia. Once on board we were told by smart uniformed officers to proceed to the upper deck. Men had to precede women up the staircase to the reception area, where we were greeted by the Queen and the Duke and all the royal children. When everyone was finally on board, the Duke walked over to Ruth and me and wanted to know what an Englishman was doing in the Shetland Isles. We chatted for some time and explained our role in the life of the mission. We then eased our way through the crowd, which must have numbered two hundred or so, found the Baptist minister and told him of our conversation with the Duke. He looked at me with a grin and said, "You may have spoken to the Duke but do you realise you have just pushed past the back of the Queen?" He was right; I hadn't realised it was her. We quickly moved on.

The royal children were causing a lot of amusement among the crowd as they told home secrets about their parents. The Duke, who must have overheard their conversation, sent them packing to their rooms.

Part of the celebration was the review of the fishing fleet. This went on for a couple of hours. The Queen was determined to acknowledge every boat, even though most of the guests had become a little bored with the review and started chatting amongst themselves. Our visit to Britannia caused quite a stir at the mission head office. Sir William Duthie was very upset with me for going on board Britannia in a lounge suit. He made it very plain to me that I had stepped out of line by not wearing a uniform. I feel they were annoyed because the invitation had come to me and not the head office executive. Perhaps they were right, but it was great fun for Ruth and me.

The winter days were short and one longed for the long days of summer. The New Year was celebrated by an annual event called 'Up Helly Aa'. This provided an opportunity for every section of the community to forget the 'winter blues' and join in a light-hearted procession behind a full-sized Viking boat around the town. I had to learn that the Shetlanders' roots go back to Norway and not Scotland. The boat was built by the Guizer Jarl Squad who were dressed in the striking uniforms of the Viking warriors. It was a great honour to be in the squad and they took pride in the detail of the uniform. During the day, the procession went from hall to hall for entertainment and drinks. The mission was one of their rest places, and fortunately they were all quite sober when they arrived. A few of the committee associated with the mission raised eyebrows at my decision to allow the procession to visit the mission. Thankfully they behaved themselves and appreciated the free coffee. They were a great bunch of men.

In the evening the parade was joined by hundreds of people carrying lighted torches made from tarred rags on the end of poles. It made a fantastic sight as the procession made its way to the central park accompanied by loud music and very noisy Shetlanders. Late in the evening, the boat was hauled to the centre of the park. The members of the procession then hurled their torches into the boat. Soon it became a blazing inferno. The beautiful Viking ship that had taken hundreds of hours to build was soon reduced to a pile of ashes. It was great fun and I recorded it all on my little cine camera.

These were great days and everyone in Shetland knew about the mission and its staff. You felt like a big fish in a small pond. Jimmy and Eileen, my assistant and his wife, lived in the apartment below us and when England was playing Scotland at football we thumped the floor when we scored and he hit the ceiling when they scored. He once rang me at 3am saying the Northern Lights could be seen from the lounge window. It was a fantastic sight, and Ruth joined me, kneeling by the radiator and enjoying the show.

However, constant change was part of life and before long,

the postman delivered yet another letter telling us we had to move.

The first letter came saying that Aberdeen was the next on the list. However, this was followed by another letter stating that we were being sent to Ayr. This was a relief as I had no illusions about going to a trawler port as the boss. Grimsby was bad enough, but I understood that Aberdeen was worse. It really was a terrible wrench leaving Lerwick behind, especially for Tina, as she had such a great bunch of school friends who spent endless hours together making and selling things for worthy causes. She did not want to move, and it was a sad day for her. However, little did I know that many years later we would be back in Shetland to witness Clifford being inducted into the post of mission Superintendent.

Chapter 7

Ayr

So we arrived in Ayr. The man who had charge of the mission was not at all pleased to see me for he was the one being sent to Aberdeen. The building was in the fish market area and only a few steps from the quayside, an ideal situation. The canteen was well used and once again, the snooker table was in constant use by the dock workers. It had a screened-off section for the chapel, along with a television room, a small lounge and two bedrooms for fishermen. Our apartment was at the top of the building, and the views over the sea to the Isle of Arran were just fantastic. Our time in Ayr proved to be another turning point in our spiritual experience. God had His purpose in allowing us to come to this mission and it was one of the most rewarding times.

During the early days at Ayr I had to visit the local railway station. I visited Smith's bookstall and bought Time Magazine. The front cover picture carried the story of the Jesus movement in California. I immediately found a seat in the local café, sat down and read the amazing account of God's work amongst the hippies of California. Deep inside of me I sensed a resounding "Yes" to everything I read. Thousands upon thousands of young people experiencing a new life in Jesus; joyful, spontaneous worship on the beaches, hundreds being baptised in the sea, hands raised in worship and young worship leaders writing new songs with fresh upbeat music to accompany it. New churches were being formed as the traditional ones refused to accept the new converts. Many leaders actually felt threatened by them. Healings and speaking in tongues were regular experiences amongst them.

Up to this time I had frowned on the emotionalism of Pentecostal churches, although I had a sneaking feeling that they had something that I didn't. I think God was gently taking us forward in our journey of faith. I sat in this railway café totally absorbed by this report of changed lives of so many Californian hippies. This fresh move of the Spirit among these young people was to become a movement that went around the world and little did I know that in the years to come I would be in meetings in the UK that were to equal the blessing experienced in California.

As I left Ayr railway station I knew that a new day had dawned for me and that in ways I didn't understand, I was a part of this fresh move of the Holy Spirit. In the years to come I was to stand on the very beach in California where these baptisms had taken place.

The early days at Ayr proved to be a little frustrating as there were no 'Nightcap' meetings or groups for the ladies to attend. We had a serious shortage of staff and I had to do much of the cleaning in the mission. Well do I remember the day when I took a mop and hurled it at the wall in sheer frustration. I didn't join the mission to do this mundane work, or so I reasoned. My attitude was wrong and certainly not commendable. It did not help that Ruth was in bed with the flu, so at this time I had the responsibility of looking after Ruth and the family and I am not a good cook as our children will tell you. I was not a happy man at this time. Where was God in all this? We really didn't want to be in Ayr. If only we were back in Lerwick life would be so much better, we reasoned. God, however, had better plans.

Ruth had been asked to speak at the local Baptist church for the Women's World Day of Prayer. Her allotted subject was, 'In His will is our peace', hardly the best subject when we were questioning our posting to Ayr. While recovering from the flu she had begun to read a Catherine Marshall book called 'Something More'. The final chapter came as a real challenge when Catherine wrote about the 'Prayer of Relinquishment'. Ruth asked herself if she could do this. Here was a real challenge, but like the author of the book, she eventually said, "I accept the situation, and I'm ready and trust you, Lord, to work it all out." The days went by; Ruth spoke at the ladies' meeting and I got over my mini rebellion. I recruited more staff, which enabled me to get out into the harbour area, and life returned to normal. All this just as Christmas was approaching, which meant the distribution of Christmas parcels to retired fishermen.

Sitting in my office one day, I had an internal call from the canteen staff to say that the Rev. Dr. Nelson Gray was at the counter and wanted to speak to me. Never having heard of him before I wondered what he wanted. Perhaps he was a local Church of Scotland minister wanting to welcome me to his parish. I was soon to find out he was the Director of the Scottish Religious Department of ITV.

He started by asking if I could spare him some time to discuss a proposed Christmas service. I can remember wondering why on earth he had approached me, the superintendent of a station of the Fishermen's Mission. He soon came to the point saying he would very much like to use the mission for a live TV Christmas Eve service. My mouth just dropped open in amazement, "Help," I thought. "We don't even have a congregation here. Why didn't he come to me in Lerwick where we had a full house every Sunday?" Nonetheless, all the time my heart was saying "Yes! Yes! Yes!" In no way would I mention the problems needing to be overcome in case he changed his mind. Only a few weeks before I was cleaning out the toilets and throwing mops about. Now we were being offered a role that would take the Fishermen's Mission into the front room of the nation. I felt like saying, "This must be a joke. Please go away," but no; there he was in my office saying, "We must work together to make this broadcast the best ever." How could I say no? What an amazing, thrilling opportunity this was, I could hardly contain my excitement and longed to tell the family upstairs. There were big issues to be considered, such as where the congregation would come from. I didn't know anyone in the locality. To whom and where should I turn? The answer was to be found in the 'Christmas parcel list'. A letter was hastily sent to these retired fishermen inviting them and their families to the Christmas broadcast. To my relief, nearly everyone wanted to attend. On instructions from Rev. Gray, the invitation also included the request "Please do not wear your Sunday best hats." He knew that people loved to dress up for the services and 'Sunday hats' wouldn't fit the image of a fishing community.

The 24th of December arrived. The technicians took the entire building over. The cables, lights, and TV cameras they installed totally transformed the place. Nelson Gray and his team were reassuring and full of confidence. "The evening is going to be the best ever," he said. None of the family had ever seen anything like this before and we were getting a little apprehensive as the day went by. I need not have worried about a congregation as fishermen and families soon filled the building. The instruction given to the ladies was obeyed. No 'Sunday best hats' were to be seen.

I had informed the police of the event. I knew from past experience that drunk fishermen had a habit of turning up when least expected. I was right, one did. For a change I didn't have to deal with him.

An hour or so before the broadcast I took a long walk by the harbour. It was full of boats which had returned home for the Christmas break. It was a bitterly cold night and standing right at the end of the quay and looking out to sea I knew I couldn't do this on my own. I needed all the help I could get, so I began to pray, "Thank you Lord for this amazing opportunity, I can't wait to get started; use me for your glory." I added, "Sorry for complaining about coming to Ayr; you know best." Then as I anticipated the evening's broadcast, I could hardly refrain from shouting out, "Yes, Yes, Yes." What an opportunity! – something I could only dream of doing. I just wished my mother and father could have been present. To be the preacher in a live Christmas broadcast was beyond my wildest dreams. This was a 'one-off' experience never to be repeated. My feelings were a mixture of, "Hey this is going to be fun,"

"This is serious and people need to know of God's love to mankind in the birth of a Saviour," and "Help, will I blow it?" It amazed me that Nelson Gray had asked me to preach, for we had only met a few weeks ago. Eventually I made my way back to the mission. Several TV vans were parked outside. Lights illuminated the building and more importantly, crowds of people were arriving for the broadcast.

Nelson and I took up our position outside the building and he was about to speak to the camera welcoming everyone to the service when to his horror he realised he had mislaid his cue cards. There was panic all round. "Ruth!" I shouted. "Do you know where he put them?" "Yes," she replied, "I think I last saw them in the apartment by the telly." "Tina," she shouted, "just run and get them!" With seconds to spare, Nelson had his cue cards in his hands and calmly welcomed everyone to the 'inn from the sea' as he put it. "Well, Superintendent Powell, let's go inside. Like the stable at Bethlehem this mission is a place of warmth and refuge. Let's see what is going on." So we walked inside as the congregation were singing the first carol.

The children were all standing by the billiard table. Nelson interviewed them by asking what they expected Father Christmas to bring them. Clifford replied, in a broad Scottish accent, "I want a game of Battling Tops." Richard said, "I want a chemistry set," to which Nelson replied with a laugh, "Well, do you want to blow up the mission?" Tina read the well-known Christmas story in Luke. Of course she was nervous, but her Scottish accent came across strong and clear. To steady any nerves, she had inserted a handwritten slip of paper into her Bible, which said, "Don't be afraid of their faces; you can't see them." (She has this scrap of paper to this day.) She read perfectly. We were so proud of them all. After their involvement, we sent them up to bed and heard them running up the stairs and along the landing, no doubt to watch the rest of the service on the TV.

Moira Anderson sang, 'As I walked down the road to Bethlehem'. The tough fishermen's choir from Peterhead sang, 'Fierce and wild the storm was raging'. They made it sound as if we were in a force nine gale. This was followed by one of the Duncan boys sharing the story of the loss of their father George overboard. The tragedy was still fresh in everyone's mind. The traditional carols were sung and I concluded the service by saying that as the shepherds made haste to see the baby Jesus, so the men of the sea had returned home for Christmas to their loved ones. Tonight 'Emmanuel' is still with us and He invites us to receive Him into our hearts and lives.

Ruth sat in the front row. Her love, support and smile were so reassuring. She has always been there to encourage and support me. Suddenly it was all over. Nelson and the TV crew said the show was fantastic: no doubt relieved no-one (including me) had messed it up. One member of the crew became a Christian as a result of the broadcast. The choir then faced a three-hour journey back to Peterhead. Moira Anderson, a well-known TV personality and local resident, chatted away to her fans. We went to bed exhausted. What an evening! – especially considering we hadn't wanted to come to Ayr in the first place. I am so glad, with hindsight, that we did come.

Within a few days, life was back to normal. The canteen was full and a man was entertaining everyone on the piano. He was a good performer. Could he be the answer to a question I had begun to ask myself? Why not hold a Sunday Nightcap in the little chapel? We had packed it out for the Christmas broadcast, so maybe some would come again. I needed a pianist. He was a warm lovable character – not a fisherman but the Vice Commodore of the Ayr Yachting Club. It wasn't difficult to ask him, and to my surprise he immediately agreed and he would also bring his wife and two children. I kept saying "Yes! Yes! Yes!" to myself as I went upstairs and told Ruth the good news. After distributing some publicity around the harbour and fish market area, we found ourselves with a small congregation of twenty people for our first Nightcap. Tom the pianist was in good form and the singing was excellent. After the meeting, he said to me that he was delighted to play the piano but warned me emphatically not to involve him in anything else. Of course I was thrilled to have him. I noticed that he didn't use the music book, although he knew the hymns and how to play them. Everyone wanted to sing along with him. After three weeks, he phoned to say he couldn't make it on Sunday, and neither did he come into the mission during that week to entertain his mates. Another two weeks went by, and still no Tom. Early one morning we had a phone call. It was Tom who was upset and wanted to talk, so could I come round? "Tom," I said, "Give me a few minutes and I will be with you." On my arrival he was full of his story, but first he apologised for missing the meetings.

Then he began a story that took my breath away. He started by saying, "You don't know me, Tony, and you have no understanding of my past life, and of course why should you?" His wife was sitting beside him, obviously very moved by his tears. He was a broken man and wanted us to know all about it. His father was a well-known Brethren evangelist and during Tom's teenage years he had accompanied his father playing the piano at various evangelistic meetings. Over the years the relationship became very strained. He left home and Tom joined the Navy and said goodbye to his Christian upbringing. He lived as all naval ratings do – enjoying life, living for the moment and taking no interest in spiritual matters. He was involved in several near-death experiences, on one occasion being severely injured. After a few years, he left the Navy and went to medical school. This did not suit him, so he left and worked for a drug company – soon rising to a senior position.

He had a love of boats and was part of the local yacht club. He and his crew often came into the mission for refreshments. On Christmas Eve, he had watched the service with his neighbours and loved every minute of it. He told me that they toasted me with a glass of whisky after I preached. Perhaps that is why he didn't have a problem with me asking him to play at the Nightcap. However, he didn't bargain for the Holy Spirit tapping him on the shoulder and saying, "I have missed you." So for three weeks he visited friends. He was a man on the run and didn't know where to go. The incident that brought him to his knees took place one day when he was staying in a hotel in Aberdeen and could not go out for a walk. With nothing to do and no papers to read, he picked up the Gideon Bible and opened it at random. There before him was the promise of God that He would do a new thing for him and the former life was forgiven. All he had to do was to receive God's unconditional love. So this wonderful man got down on his knees and asked God to do that. As he prayed, he was totally overwhelmed by the presence of God.

All this took place in the early hours of the morning so without going back to sleep he booked out of the hotel and made for home. His wife Muriel was surprised to see him home so early but within a short time she joined him on her knees beside the bed and together they committed themselves to their newly-found Friend and Saviour Jesus. Ruth and I were overwhelmed by their story, and could not have been happier to have played a part in it. So we began a journey with them together as God unfolded His plans for their lives. Tom never missed another Nightcap meeting and we must have seen each other several times during the weeks that followed.

The love of his life was the sea and sailing and he was in the process of buying a brand-new yacht, but he questioned whether this was appropriate in view of his rediscovered faith and Sunday worship. He had put down a substantial deposit on the yacht and it was to be the biggest and the best in the Ayr Club. We set a date and if it was not delivered by that time he would not take it. The months went by and the promised delivery date for the yacht had been agreed by the Glasgow head office. However, it arrived one day later than the agreed date. With gritted teeth he wrote to the company saying he no longer wanted the boat. Needless to say there was a mini explosion in a swanky head office in Glasgow. Threatening letters came from lawyers waving signed contracts but Tom refused to budge, saying that God would restore every penny of his deposit. Amazingly his new-found faith sustained him. His father and family said he was being rather extreme and asked where God was in it all. He proposed that Tom should employ a solicitor and fight for his money back. The days and weeks went by and one day a letter dropped on the front doormat with a cheque containing the full deposit he had paid all those months ago. This was followed by his dramatic resignation from his well-paid job, the selling of his house and contents, along with his much-loved yacht, and the bold decision to start training for the Christian ministry at the McMaster University in Toronto. We had one amazing time with Tom and his dear wife Muriel and the boys. I remember saying goodbye to them at Prestwick Airport and Tom turning to me and saying, "I recall saying to you, Tony, when you first asked me to play the piano that I wouldn't want to be involved in anything else than playing the piano, but now look at me and the family!" We knelt on the hard marble floor of the airport and with arms around each other, committed this couple who we had come to love to our Heavenly Father. It was sad to say goodbye even to a man who was clearly following a path directed by a very loving Heavenly Father. Ruth and I had learned a lot from our friendship with Tom and Muriel and their two boys.

Our huge lounge window overlooked the road, the harbour wall and scores of fishing boats. Many enjoyable hours were spent watching all the activity. The children had a great time playing with fish boxes and inventing all sorts of adventures. One day I was watching Richard running around the harbour area when he suddenly dashed for home. To my horror I could see a car coming down the road just as he was about to run between two sheds directly in front of the oncoming car. I could only scream at the plate-glass window in front of me and watch helplessly as he bounced off the side of the car. A second earlier and he would have been in front of the car and I dread to think what could have happened to him. A very shaken man slammed on his brakes and rushed up to him. I was soon on the scene, and picked up Richard, shaking and somewhat bruised. The driver recovered in the mission. Richard and I both recovered upstairs in the apartment. At times like these he found comfort in laying down with his head on the ample side of our Labrador dog. We could only hug them both and thank God for preserving him.

The annual fundraising event on the fish market had its moment of embarrassment for the wife of Sir William Duthie, who had accompanied him for the opening ceremony. They had just left the mission and were walking across the road to the Sale of Work when to our amazement her pink bloomers fell to her ankles and she was unable to walk any further. The whole party had to stop and she coolly said to me, "Turn the other way, young man," stepped neatly out of the offending underwear and hid them in her handbag. I'm not sure if our children witnessed this but if they did they never told us. I know I shall never forget those 'rice bags' as Ruth called them.

Ruth wanted to start a ladies' group. I had come across a list of fifty names and addresses of women in the office so I sent them an invitation to a midweek meeting. To our surprise, nearly everyone came, including the current mayor's wife. We just couldn't believe the turnout. They were intrigued how we got their addresses. I showed them the list giving their names and addresses followed by a number between 70 and 100. One bright lady knew exactly what the relationship was between the number and the person. Apparently they had attended the Sale of Work on the fish market and had entered a game to guess the number of peas in a jar. Of course the group became known as 'the Pea Ladies' although not everyone appreciated the title.

"Have you read your daughter's letter in the local paper?" a number of folk attached to the mission asked me one day. We had not. The letter was from her heart and made us realise for the first time how hard it had been for Tina to leave her friends in Lerwick. The letter said very plainly that she and the family had moved from mission to mission and she wasn't happy about it. It made painful reading. I think this letter finished up on the General Secretary's desk in London, for I know that his wife was very upset about it. After we left the mission, the practice of moving families so frequently was changed and family life was given greater consideration.

A most unpleasant character wanted my attention in the office one day while his mate walked upstairs and calmly opened our apartment door with the intention of burgling us. Thor (meaning God of Thunder) was roused from his bed in the kitchen and shot down the passageway barking and snarling at the intruder. The man talking to me suddenly lost interest in the conversation and he and his mate disappeared out of the front door with Thor at their heels.

Jim Taylor was the minister of the Ayr Baptist Church

and he and his family became good friends. It was he who introduced us to camping and we enjoyed several holidays together. He was a very good preacher and his church was full every Sunday. On one occasion he asked people from the congregation to pray as part of the time of worship. There was a very long silence, and a few muffled coughs from the congregation. Who would be the first? This was something that was out of the usual and nobody was inclined to launch into spontaneous prayer or praise. Most of the congregation were studying their footwear. Suddenly, to our amazement Tina boldly stood to her feet, and gave an impromptu prayer. She was only about ten at the time, I felt like giving her a clap. Maybe on the strength of her outstanding prayer, Jim Taylor then decided to invite me to preach one Sunday. He must have thought if Tina could pray like this, then her father should prove his worth. On reflection I don't think my nerves were as steady as Tina's. She was able to stand up in church without preparation and speak out her prayer but I discovered I lacked the same confidence, I needed a helping hand. I was currently reading the sermons of Peter Marshall which I found truly inspiring. Surely, I thought, they would bless the congregation at the Ayr Baptist Church as much as they had blessed me, and what he had to say was far more interesting than anything I could have said. So Sunday morning arrived and I delivered a word-perfect Peter Marshall sermon to a full church. The custom in the church was for the preacher to say good morning to everyone as they left the church, and I did so, glowing with relief that it was all over. It was a pleasure to receive lots of warm handshakes and generous thanks. Suddenly the truth came out when a bright young man said, "I too have read Peter Marshall," and his penetrating look said it all. I am sure Peter Marshall would have forgiven me but I took a long time to forgive myself. I could hardly bring myself to talk to Ruth and the family as we made our way home. Her attitude was, "I told you so, Tony. When will you learn to believe in yourself?" She was right – if only I had listened.

Chapter 8

Fraserburgh

Sure enough, before long another letter from our wonderful head office landed on our doormat, saying next stop Fraserburgh! Actually, Ruth had prepared us all and said that the Lord had shown her a scripture saying we would be in the next mission for three years and the final year would be a tremendous time of blessing. I had no problems in going to Fraserburgh. In fact when we first considered joining the mission it would have been my first choice. Just a few years before we arrived in Fraserburgh, the head office had closed the ancient building and built a new mission on the dockside. There was much feeling and frustration amongst the members. However, everything soon settled down and the people continued to support the work in the new building, complete with all the excellent facilities needed to serve the fishing community. The Sunday Nightcap continued to be well attended .

Walking around the harbour one day I saw some old fishermen sitting in a car chatting amongst themselves. As I passed by they wound down the window and one of them called out, "You are the new 'mission man', are you?" Considering I was in uniform it wasn't too difficult a deduction on their part. "Well, Superintendent, you need to know that the first year you will be idolised, the second criticised, and the third year scandalised." An interesting comment, I thought – but how do you reply to that? I could only shrug my shoulders and walk on. All I could hear was muffled laughter as I walked away. As far as they were concerned they had made their point and I had to live with it. Thank God it was never true, for we went from strength to strength and the final year, as Ruth had said, was the best ever in the mission.

The time in Fraserburgh was dominated by events that were either tragic or enjoyable. The tragic events were heart-breaking. I found myself in situations that I never had to deal with in any other mission. During the three years in Fraserburgh I had to break the news to no less than thirty wives that their husbands had been drowned at sea. After a while I dreaded the phone going at night. "Surely not another boat, Ruth," I would say as I went to the phone. The very act of parking the mission car outside a house when everyone knew a boat was late home from sea sent fear running through the household. Sometimes the Provost accompanied me but other times I was on my own. I would always pray with the wives and offer practical and financial help through the mission and other seafaring charities. During the following months they were often visited by me, the 'mission man'. Social work was always high on the agenda. At Christmas all the fatherless children were given presents and a party. We often had parties for fifty or more children. We also gave Christmas parcels to retired fishermen and widows. This of course could run into hundreds of calls in villages along the coast, where everyone was a Buchan or a Strachan, especially when some of the houses had no numbers on the doors. One cottage in Inverallochy was known as 'two and a half Gibb'.

On one awful occasion an entire crew was lost at sea. A memorial service was held in the Muckle Kirk and attended by over a thousand people. I took a part in the service. The whole town was in mourning. As someone remarked, this is the price of our fish and chips. What a price!! Most of the men were in their twenties and thirties. The usual practice was to put up a brass memorial plate in the mission for men lost at sea. There are now so many in the Fraserburgh Mission a memorial room has been set up which is almost too traumatic to enter.

We opened the mission every Sunday at 11pm till 2am. This had been the practice established by my predecessor. Traditionally the fishing fleet didn't leave the harbour until 'the back of Sunday', in other words after midnight. This was because until recent years the God-fearing community thought it would offend the Almighty if they worked in any way on the Sabbath. So we opened the canteen and did a roaring trade. A lot of the men needed last-minute items before going to sea for the week. So gutting knives, rubber gloves, bags of sweets and cigarettes and many other items were passed over the counter to these tired-looking men. I can't imagine what Ruth's grandfather would have thought of her selling cigarettes, and on a Sunday at that, although one would hope they would appreciate her commitment in helping out in the early hours of the morning. Bill, Maggie and Godfrey were on duty with us and we were a happy team.

My most enjoyable task was to go down to the harbour wall in the mission car loaded with bundles of magazines. These were made up of Readers Digest, National Geographic magazines, paperbacks and Christian literature. I would hurl these bundles some thirty feet or so onto the decks of the passing boats. The men were often waiting for them and a big cheer went up if they succeeded in catching the bundle. On one occasion a man broke his finger catching the bundle, so the boat returned to the harbour a few minutes later and I took him to hospital. He missed a fishing trip that week.

It was a moving sight to watch the ropes being cast off from floodlit boats. The air would be full of the smell of diesel fumes from the noisy engines. The screech of seagulls overhead nearly drowned the faint farewells of loved ones. It was a very emotional time. Soon the boats were just dots of light in the inky blackness of the night. Car engines started and wives and parents returned home hoping their loved ones would have a good catch and safe return. If they did well, the rewards were great. It was a boom time in the fishing industry in the sixties and seventies with the deckhands earning hundreds of pounds a week. Some skippers were millionaires. Two weeks of their earnings would have paid my annual salary.

During the summer months, the Camerons, from a Pentecostal church from Peterhead, would come to the harbour during these late Sunday evenings and sing gospel songs through a very loud public address system. They were great musicians and singers and I believe the men appreciated them. My favourite was called 'the lighthouse song' which could be heard all over the busy harbour area. It was appreciated by the fishermen but not the local residents, so sadly they stopped coming.

Leaving the harbour one Sunday night I returned to the mission to be told that a drunk fisherman had fallen into the water trying to board his boat. It was a bitterly cold night and when I got to the scene he had already been pulled out of the water and was lucky to be alive. He was in no fit state to go to sea and the skipper was pleased to see the back of him. A very dirty, smelly, oily, subdued man was taken back to the mission for a hot shower and dry clothes. I went off to make a few phone calls when suddenly there were screams coming from the canteen. The ladies on duty had disappeared into a cupboard at the back of the kitchen because our drunk friend had become rather boisterous under the shower. He had wrapped himself in a blanket and was dancing half-naked around the canteen and not too bothered if his blanket fell to the floor. Several other fishermen were 'black affronted' that this should happen in the mission and they escorted him out of the building. Maybe they threw him out, I don't know. The ladies then emerged from their hiding place, it was quite amusing really and not at all unusual.

The 'back of Sunday' was one of the highlights of the week. On another occasion a young fisherman came in covered with blood. He had just driven his car through the plate-glass window of the local car showroom. He then panicked and dashed into our building. The police were called and he was soon sorted out. There were several other instances of men falling into the harbour but none quite like our friend above.

We went to a local church on Sunday mornings. The minister, although a very friendly man, suddenly changed when he mounted the pulpit steps so our usual comment when entering the building was, "Are we going to get a bashing or a blessing?" If it was the former we would play some very upbeat music on our return and dance around the apartment. Of course, our main Sunday involvement was the Nightcap which gave me the responsibility and pleasure of sharing a range of issues that faith in Jesus could affect and change. What a privilege. The meetings just grew and grew during the three years in Fraserburgh.

The long-standing tradition in all mission services was to conclude the service by singing the hymn 'Eternal Father'. This was very acceptable to me and I know it was appreciated by all who had family at sea. However, there were some occasions when I felt it detracted from the sermon. I sometimes needed to close the meeting with a prayer of commitment. On one memorable occasion I asked our pianist, Miss Watson, a retired Mission Superintendent, not to play 'Eternal Father', and instead I would lead into an appeal for people to respond to the Gospel invitation. This lady had served in the mission for over fifty years and had little idea what I was talking about. Nothing was going to stop her playing the traditional hymn. As I came to the end of my sermon and was preparing to lead into an appeal, she suddenly started playing 'Eternal Father'. Of course I could not stop her. I am sure the Holy Spirit understood both motives, hers and mine, but I was nevertheless a shade frustrated. I know that faith grew in many lives during our time in Fraserburgh, some, I believe, for the first time. Miss Watson's loyalty to the work was amazing and she taught Ruth the need to keep short accounts with everyone she ministered to, especially during those times when relationships were difficult.

The Nightcap was mostly attended by the older generation. Head office dictated it started at 8pm so as not to conflict with local church services. Unfortunately it meant that most of the active fishermen were at home getting ready to go to sea. The retired men and wives made up most of the congregation. One man in particular just loved the meetings and throughout the sermon he kept up a constant "Imen." I knew what he meant but one youngster said, "Why does he keep on telling everyone he is in? We can all see him." Billy was a lovely man and very well known in the fishing community, and it was encouraging to hear his "Amen" from time to time.

One Saturday night the washing machine in our apartment above the canteen suffered a burst pipe. It must have been running for hours. When we came downstairs in the morning the entire building was two inches deep in water. That evening at the Nightcap the request for favourite hymns gave our boys a unique opportunity to shout out, 'Showers of Blessing', 'Will your anchor hold?' and 'Let some droppings fall on me'. Ruth was hiding her face behind her hymn book but we could all hear her muffled laughter. For obvious reasons we had tried to keep quiet about the accident. However, the boys couldn't keep quiet and their requests for seafaring hymns kept on coming. 'Wide, wide as the ocean', 'Rivers of living water', and other sea hymns. I think our young family was quite an attraction for the 'Nightcappers'. I know the boys loved the cakes and biscuits after the meeting. When all was finished, the chairs had to be cleared away and once again it became a canteen. We only had an hour or so before opening for the 'back of Sunday fishermen'. Sunday was a very full day.

The canteen proved to be a good meeting point for the young fishermen's wives. During the week the place seemed to be swarming with prams and babies at times. Tea must have been drunk by the gallon. They were a great bunch of ladies and very soon Ruth had them all enrolled in her young wives' group. They met in the upstairs fishermen's lounge and the children played in the bedrooms when not in use by shipwrecked fishermen. The whole event was just amazing. Within a few weeks the room was packed to capacity. Her initial concern was whether her brief 'Christian Chat' would be acceptable. She was very nervous about this. However, there really was no need to worry about it. In latter years she was told by the girls that it was the highlight of the afternoon sessions. Ruth was really gifted in this ministry but if anyone told her so, she would say how inadequate she felt. She just loved the girls and had a lot of fun with them. She even created a choir who became sufficiently proficient to sing at several social events dressed in mini tartan skirts. Ruth recalls several young wives saying to her that they were singing hymns that were not relevant for them. Her quick reply was, "They can be: make a step of faith." Over the three years that lay ahead many did. They were great days.

Not only did the young wives and children use the building during the day but so also did retired fishermen. The evenings were usually quiet, so we had the idea of starting an indoor bowls club, as we had plenty of space on the canteen floor. So with a modest outlay of funds, a carpet and bowls were purchased and many a happy evening was spent with a great bunch of men.

As time went by we ventured out into more Saturday night events for all of the community. There was a lot of talent amongst them all so to arrange a ceilidh wasn't too demanding. Godfrey, my assistant, entertained everyone with a good performance of 'Albert and the Lion', in a broad Yorkshire accent. Katie Buchan read poems in the strong Fraserburgh tongue. Solos good and bad came at a great rate. Every item was followed by really thunderous applause. Then of course we had 'Tattie an' Herring' suppers. Everyone just loved these. It had been the staple diet for many past generations but had been largely forgotten by the present affluent fishing community. Everyone wanted a reminder of this past delicacy. Herring were in abundant supply and free for the mission. Mashed potatoes, bread and butter plus a mug of tea were also easy to supply. The smell would linger in the building for days after the event. This basic meal was followed by some light entertainment which could always be guaranteed to fill the building whenever we wanted to put it on. There came a point when we had to issue tickets for the Saturday night specials. It was fun. Ruth and I would have really loved to have put on a barn dance but the tradition of the mission forbade that. Instead we decorated the building like a barn, complete with bales of straw, candles in bottles, cartwheels, old lanterns, in fact anything that would look at home in a barn, but, no dancing, which was a pity, for a lot of the young folk would have loved it. Even so, it was most enjoyable and the evening concerts provided opportunities for talent.

You may well ask why all this involvement in activities that had no evangelistic content. I would argue against this by considering the Lord's attendance at parties. For too long, the Christian life has consisted of meetings and more meetings. Without doubt, times of corporate worship and ministry must be high on our agenda but to ignore times of relaxation or even to ban them in the church is not in line with the life and teaching of Jesus. "I am come," said Jesus, "to give you life, and life more abundantly." The important side effect of these social evenings was the deepening of relationships between everyone. We all need to observe the life of Jesus. He built relationships to an amazing level of loyalty and love. Let us endeavour to live life at the same level, even if our attempts can be frustrating and difficult at times.

I knew we were under constant observation from many people in the Fraserburgh community. I was quite shocked one day to read in the local paper that, "The Powells are leaving the mission this weekend for a holiday in London, we all wish them well." This article came as a result of chatting informally to a reporter on the steps of the mission. I felt like a big fish in a very small pond. This was never the case when we were in London; rather the opposite.

"It's about time you made a trip with us, then you will really find out what life is like at sea. Are you up to it?" So spoke a friendly fisherman whom I had come to know as I walked around the dockside. How could I refuse a trip? To chicken out would destroy my credibility. At heart I really wanted to make a trip, but I was rather concerned about seasickness. I knew that our head office would certainly approve. So instead of throwing bundles of magazines on board the boats, one evening I found myself waving goodbye to a rather anxious Ruth at the 'back of Sunday'.

Our destination was the Outer Hebrides to pair trawl for herring. I was on board a small boat with a crew of five, which was well past its 'sell by date'. The living, cooking and sleeping quarters were all in the same room. It really was very, very basic. I had a top bunk with plenty of bedding and I was reasonably comfortable. About two in the morning I eventually dropped off to sleep aided by the motion of the boat and the throb of the engine.

Night passed. "Are you up for a decent breakfast, Tony?" asked a young deckhand. "Pile it on, no problem," I said. I was hungry and ready for the day's activity. At that time we were steaming somewhere off the coast of Caithness near John O'Groats. The crew slept and worked in the same clothes all week. I sat down to a full plate of eggs, bacon, fried bread, plus a huge mug of tea. Some of the men were already on deck getting the nets ready. As I sat down to eat I slowly became aware of the strong smell of diesel fuel, body odour and cooking. It was wicked. For some reason, the combination of these smells created a response in my feet. I began to feel a strange tingling sensation in my feet that gradually crept up my legs. This feeling combined with the swaying of the boat soon reached my stomach. The previously enticing plate of food in front of me became untouchable. Pushing the plate aside I climbed the narrow ladder leading to the deck and threw up over the side of the boat. I had already been told by the skipper that if I was seasick they would not be turning back. "No one," he said, "has ever died of seasickness." I knew they expected to be at sea for at least four days and intended landing the catch at Oban. Even if no one had ever died of seasickness, after three days of agony I began to wonder if I would be the first victim. It really was a nightmare experience never to be forgotten. For some reason, I had brought a bunch of grapes with me and they were the only food I ate for four days. The weather continued to deteriorate and when I did venture into the wheelhouse to watch the action on deck I had to hold onto anything I could grab to avoid injury. My admiration of the bravery and skills of these men rose dramatically as I peered out of a rain-soaked window. Huge waves were crashing over slippery decks, taut cables, and screaming winches. Slippery fish were waiting to be trod on. Accidents were just waiting to happen. Added to this, the thousands of herring were being pumped into the hold as the boats came together to deliver up their catch. What a sight! All this took place during the early hours of the morning under swaying floodlighting suspended on cables over the working area. From time to time the skipper would open the window and bellow down instructions to his crew.

At one stage, the boats drew alongside each other. The rise and fall between the boats at times was ten feet or so. To my amazement the men would leap from one boat to another. One slip and that would be the end of them, for the water was bitterly cold and the boats would never be able to rescue them, because the huge net between the boats would have made it impossible. The hymn we so often sang at the mission 'For those in peril on the sea' took on a fresh meaning. These men were the heroes of the deep. I would have loved to have ventured on deck to get a real feel of a fisherman's work but a stern word from the skipper forbade it. A wise decision.

The catch was a good one. I was relieved to hear the skipper say that tomorrow he would be landing it at Ullapool. I

recall my good friend Jimmy Ralph who was once a fisherman and now a mission man saying that in the old days
they called herring 'silver darlings' and when they had a
good catch they would throw themselves over the catch
shouting "Whoopee," no doubt with joy and relief. It must
have been quite a sight. The 'Tattie an' Herring' suppers
at the mission took on a whole new meaning after that.

What a relief when the next day arrived. It certainly could
not have come quickly enough, as Ullapool came into
sight, seasickness left me and home beckoned. However,
the skipper, not realising my relief at seeing land, said, "We
are going out tonight, Tony, are you up to it?" My quick
answer, a very definite "No" may have surprised him. As
we drew alongside the pier I was the first to jump and feel
solid ground under my feet – at least I expected to feel solid
ground but for two days I had this unpleasant sensation of
swaying from side to side. It's the nearest I've ever felt
to being drunk. With plenty of fish lorries returning to
Fraserburgh I was soon home to a very amused family
as they heard my tale of woe. Sympathy wasn't too high
on their agenda, although humour definitely was. Maybe
I went up a notch or two in the eyes of the fishermen but
they never told me. It was my first and last trip to sea as
a novice fisherman. My work contribution to the trip was
precisely zero.

The 'fisher wifies', in Ruth's Monday night meeting
somehow got to hear we were short of money for a washing
machine. The question they put to her was "Are you
proud?" and said it with real meaning, apparently testing
her loyalty to them. They went on to say, "If you are not
proud then we can give you a job in the fish house." Ruth

rose to the challenge as she did not want to lose face in front of one hundred women in her meeting and valiantly said, "If you can give me a job for a couple of months then I would be very grateful and take the job." Little did she know what she was letting herself in for. There was no getting around the fact that our washing machine which had caused so much trouble in the past had come to the end of its days and needed replacing. My money in no way stretched to such an expense. The only answer was for Ruth to take a part-time job. The fish house turned out to be a corrugated tin hut with concrete flooring which was continually swimming in water. In the hut were a number of tubs full of herring that needed to be gutted and then put into tubs of brine. The first job was to squeeze the herring guts into a large bowl in the centre of the table. These fish were then rolled up with onions and became rollmop herrings in pretty jars ready for the customers in Harrods. Ruth and all the other 'fisher wifies' were clothed in white overalls, white boots and an amazing white turban covering their hair. The whole place was a few degrees above freezing and water flowed everywhere. Ruth, once secretary in a London bank, bravely took up the challenge of the 'fisher wifies'. Perhaps I should mention that if ever the children were sick I had to mop it up, as she had a very weak stomach for this sort of thing. To her credit she stuck at it for several weeks until we had the money for the washing machine. However, the intense cold eventually got to her and she finished up with more than a mere cold in her nose. For more than one reason the work therefore came to an end. By now her hair was impregnated with a strong smell of fish and if her head was anywhere near my nose when in bed, it was not a pleasant smell. I think the fish wives were really proud of her. I know she enjoyed their company but the work was really too demanding, especially on top of the demands of her ministry in the mission. She is a woman to be proud of, and one who gained a fresh understanding and appreciation of all the women who have spent a lifetime working under such demanding conditions. They were a great bunch of ladies.

Bill, Maggie, Ella, Nannie, George Pirie and many others became good friends and spoilt our children with many special outings and treats. When it came to practical hands-on help, George was the man. He seemed to be able to turn his hand to anything. He made a buzz box for quizzes, round tables painted like wagon wheels and installed a public address system for the Nightcap. He was a good friend to the family. Ella became a special friend to Ruth and they would often get together to pray about her family situation. Sweets seemed to pour out of her handbag into the hands of our children. The staff in the canteen were headed up by Nan who did far more than she was paid for. Jean and several others worked alongside her. The whole operation could never have continued without these big-hearted people. I developed a particular liking for boiled neep (swede) and loved to take a few squares when everyone had gone home. Nan always knew a few were missing but never asked questions. Our routine consisted of frequent trips to Cash and Carry, stock taking, wages, visiting homes, too many funerals, and most importantly, being available to meet any daily needs that crossed our path.

The boys made some great friends with the sons of fisher-men and on many occasions I would see them racing around the harbour in a speed boat. I think the harbourmaster turned a blind eye to their outrageous antics.

I was given a wet -suit along with full diving equipment. Ruth loves to tell the story of when I tried it out for the first time. It was a snowy winter's day, and after ten minutes under the water I surfaced exhausted. I tried to climb onto some seaweed-covered rock. Ruth came to the rescue and nearly fell in herself. She began to panic as her feet started slipping on the seaweed. All this happened because I was exhausted after chasing a flat fish with the kitchen knife, but it had got away. The conversation in the car going home sticks in my memory. "Tony," said Ruth, "I just can't understand you. Even in the height of summer it's nearly impossible to get you into the sea, and here you are in the dead of winter, freezing cold, nearly drowning, all for the sake of a stupid six-inch flat fish." I did not know how to reply to that. I kept the wetsuit but the air bottle and mask were never seen again.

The Rev. John Chalmers asked me if Ruth and I would be responsible to take a small party of young people to a Billy Graham event in London called 'Spree 73'. I knew I could find accommodation for everyone at the Shaftesbury Christian Centre in Battersea so I immediately replied "Yes." John's request must have been of God. I had no idea that the trip would change all our lives. The Shaftesbury Mission was situated in the middle of a very ugly noisy run-down high-rise council estate. The pastor, Paul Draper, made us very welcome but could only offer us floor space in the hall on which to roll out our sleeping bags. Everyone enjoyed the week-long celebration and teaching. The evening meetings at Earls Court Stadium were packed to capacity. It was the first time that Cliff Richard sang as a committed Christian in a Billy Graham meeting.

Much to Ruth's dismay, my real interest was focused on the mission in Battersea. Could it be that this place of worship would be the link to the childhood interest created all those years ago by a London City Missioner? Every night as I returned to the mission the longing to be there grew and grew. The building was totally dwarfed by huge high-rise apartments. It could seat one hundred and fifty people, with two small adjoining rooms, a kitchen and an office. It was modern but really rather run down.

The modern three-bedroomed house next door was home to Paul Draper the pastor and two other young men. It was a typical bachelor pad. A motor bike engine lay half stripped on the lounge floor. Washing-up was piled on the draining board. If the curtains had been pulled they would not have met. A huge ugly mural covered the hall wall. Ruth took one look at the house and groaned inwardly. She made no comment and I kept my mouth shut. The week's events came to a close and she was very relieved to return home to our beautiful apartment. She had a lot of friends, loved the young wives' group and got on well with the staff in the canteen. The view of harbour life from the lounge window was stunning. What a contrast to Battersea and its high-rise apartments!

Everything we touched in the third year was a success. This was the promise God gave Ruth when we were in Ayr. The favour of God was with us: many of our friends had found a new faith and enjoyed the ministry at the mission. We felt settled and content but were also aware that another letter could arrive and we would be moved on yet again.

We had been in the mission for nine years and had been moved six times. The children had suffered, particularly Tina. She had made many friends in each port and broke her heart every time she left them behind.

A phone call from the Camerons in Peterhead came asking if I would be interested in hosting a group of young Filipino singers at our Nightcap. They would come dressed in their national costume. I could not refuse, and what a night it turned out to be! We always had a full house but this night we were packed out. They told moving stories of their conversions and God's dealing in their lives. Then followed a time of singing and dancing, which everyone loved. "Do come again," we all said. The offering was taken up. Without hesitation I gave half to the organiser who brought them along. The following week we asked a special friend to speak at the Nightcap. Her name was Jo Sully. She had been doing some outstanding medical work in Brazil, fifteen hundred miles up the Amazon river. She worked alongside my brother Laurie and his wife Sheila. Ruth and I had the highest regard for them. What a Nightcap that was as she told her stories of her life among the poor in riverside homes along the Amazon river! Another big offering was taken up and again I gave half to her cause. About this time, the young wives' choir sang at the Nightcap service. Once when conducting the choir, two powerful dog paws hit Ruth in the small of her back and sent her sprawling along the floor. Our huge Labrador dog had escaped from the apartment. Seeing

Ruth in full swing he joined in the fun. The choir stopped singing, looked on in amazement, then quickly burst into laughter as Ruth gave her dog a big hug as she sat up. Several men helped her to her feet. Our children thought it was most amusing, "Well done, mum," they told her afterwards. The third year was turning out as Ruth said it would. A lot was going on and life was very full.

During the year we had a surprise visit from the Rev. Ian Miller from head office. We enjoyed his company. He had been very good to us in the past and once lent us his car when we were in Scrabster so that I could visit Ruth in a hospital in Inverness. His visit on this occasion was not on a social basis. His plain message was that head office had become disturbed about the popularity of the Nightcap and other social events we were holding. They feared we were giving too much emphasis to this side of the ministry. Because of this, they had made a decision that no one should preach at the Nightcap for more than ten minutes and everything had to be toned down. He was extremely tactful and said that having a son in the ministry, he quite understood our enthusiasm. He then went on to say that he felt we were too big for the mission and implied we should be looking to develop our ministry elsewhere. He was a kind, gracious man and we believe he really had our best interests at heart.

It was now well over a year since our visit to Battersea and Ruth had been going through a long list of questions in her mind whether we should think in terms of leaving the mission and moving to Battersea, if the opportunity arose. Each time she asked a question in prayer, a positive answer was given. Our greatest concern was the location of the mission and the state schools the children would attend. Suddenly it was no longer an academic question. A letter arrived from Paul Draper saying that he would be leaving in a few months and going to Mauritius as a missionary and would we be interested in taking his place in Battersea? This really put us on the spot. We had to make some decisions and they were not easy ones. His letter was followed by a visit to the mission from my brother, Laurie. He just had to preach that Sunday night. (I'm sure he went on far longer than ten minutes.) He spoke about Isaac's servant who lived with the frustration that every well he dug was filled in by the enemy. Finally, in a new location he dug a well called 'Rehoboth', and as he finished the well he said, "Now the Lord has given us room, and we will flourish in the land" (Genesis 26 v 22). The sermon was for us. We needed 'room' to minister. The restrictions put on by head office were nothing more than a gentle nudge from the Lord saying it was time to move on.

The Deep Sea Mission had given Ruth and me a unique opportunity to serve a community and thereby grow in understanding both them and ourselves. We could not fault our time spent in the mission. Apart from a few occasions, we had been given the freedom to develop the use of the facilities and our ministry. The life suited Ruth and me in every way. We had given it our best and loved it. We had made great friends, especially with Jimmy and Eileen Ralph when we were in Lerwick Mission. Someone once said, "Constant change is here to stay." So with an invitation from Paul Draper to go to Battersea I wrote to the General Secretary of the Shaftesbury Society, Mr. Franklin, requesting an interview. The reply came saying, "Please present yourself at head office to talk things over."

By this time Ruth was at peace with the possible move. I left Fraserburgh with her approval, prepared to take the position if it was offered to me. The interview went well and I remember sitting in Battersea Park afterwards saying to myself and to God, "Am I really up to this?" There was nothing attractive about the prospect of living in the middle of one of the worst council estates in London with its constant noise, graffiti, crime, drugs, and air pollution, with a salary of £900 a year. With three children to raise, another question was could we really afford to come down. So, here I was a worried man sitting in Battersea Park looking out over the lake with my chin in my hands. Even to consider such a move seemed ridiculous. The previous night I had spent the evening in the mission house and it looked a mess. (Sorry Paul if you are reading this.) I could hear the sound of police sirens, planes overhead and the roar of traffic. I knew that what I was about to do would have an immense effect on the children; once again they would be leaving their friends behind. So it really was a cry for help to our Heavenly Father. I cannot say I felt a sense of peace about the move. It would be a major challenge, but I knew the answer had to be, "Yes, we are coming to Battersea."

The final days in Fraserburgh were emotional ones as we were overwhelmed by the goodwill, support and prayers of so many people we had come to love and trust. The promise given to Ruth three years ago came from Isaiah 37 v 30. The promise was, "This year eat what grows of itself, and the second year what springs from that, BUT in the third year, sow, reap and plant vineyards and eat their fruit." Our final year at Fraserburgh saw many coming to faith, especially among Ruth's young wives. We had a fantastic send-off and once again Thor, our dog, joined in the celebration.

Our nine years in the Deep Sea Mission had come to an end. Like the tide that was always a few feet from our front door, we had experienced the ebb and flow of life's surprises. There had been demanding times, but other occasions were far more pleasant. I often played the record by one of the Camerons in Peterhead. One song included the line, "If it wasn't for that lighthouse where would this good ship be?" Running a mission was like running a lighthouse. It was so good to say at the end of our time that a few ships had seen the light and found a safe and eternal harbour. It had been a privilege.

Chapter 9

Battersea

We stood at the front of our new home. We opened the door and made the first step into a world far removed from anything we had experienced before. Our worldly possessions could be contained in a few suitcases but our future as a family was in the secure hands of One who loved us more than we would ever know. The house was empty and without any curtains. Out of every window we could see towering council flats. We felt like a goldfish in a bowl.

The mission next door was in the final day of a two-week-long children's play scheme. Somewhere approaching three hundred children were catered for and the final attraction was the special appearance of Rolf Harris. Paul Draper had hired a lorry and a few musicians, including a certain Kevin, were seated on the back and toured the estate singing, playing, and waving to the crowds of children following the parade. Windows and balconies soon filled with people amazed that a TV personality was visiting their estate. The noise was overpowering with hundreds of excitable children everywhere. Many had painted faces, and some were dressed in amazing costumes. It was more than a children's event; it was a local carnival and everyone, man and dog alike, joined in the celebration. Furthermore, it was a hot, humid day and we had arrived in the middle of it all. Ruth's sister Mary arrived from her home in Sussex, eager to see our new situation. The parade came to a close just as scores of children heard that the new people had moved into the manse. The front door was one huge panel of clear glass, and soon sticky faces were pressed against the window and eyes could be seen through the letter box. Most of the children were from families which originated from the Caribbean. It was at this stage that the culture shock hit us all, and Ruth ran upstairs in tears saying, "What have we done?" Mary came to the rescue and reminded us of the age long truth: "Not by might, nor by power but by His spirit." In God's timing, all would be well; we just had to be patient.

There was much work to be done: beds had to be made, cases unpacked and food found for some very hungry children. That night we literally crawled into our beds, not simply because we were tired but also because there were no curtains on any of the windows, so a thousand eyes could see our every move if they so desired.

The doorbell rang early next morning and to our utter amazement we could see through the plain glass door that there standing on the doorstep were Bill, Maggie, Ella, Nannie and George. They had travelled down overnight all the way from Fraserburgh with a van loaded with carpets to lay on the bare boards of our house. We had absolutely no idea they were coming. The children were thrilled beyond words to hear the familiar Scottish accent in our new house which made it feel like home for the first time. What a privilege it is to have friends who really care.

They will never know how much their two-day visit meant to us. They were such a blessing; we were overwhelmed by their love.

The following Sunday was the service of our induction as the new Pastor and family at the Shaftesbury Christian Centre, Battersea. Paul warned us not to expect too many to attend, "This is not Fraserburgh, you know." I'm so glad he warned us as only twelve people turned up. Paul had asked three teenagers to sing a gospel song, but they got the giggles and ran out of the building never to be seen again. So began our twenty-seven years of ministry. An interesting start.

In those early days the ladies' group was attended by some elderly cockney ladies who had been part of the community since birth. They were usually dressed in dark clothing and wore felt hats secured by enormous pins with huge pearls on the end, along with thick stockings that always seemed to wrinkle around their ankles. Sometimes an apron could be seen under a thick winter coat. They spoke their minds and were not slow in telling you what they thought of you.

Ruth led the small meeting in our front room and for the first meeting I thought it would be appropriate if I stayed with Ruth to meet them all. The meeting had just started when one of them said, "And we don't want him in here," glaring at me over her tiny gold-rimmed glasses. She had one yellow tooth in her upper jaw which said, "I might be old but don't fool with me," she also had a rolled umbrella handy and it was in easy reach. I quickly disappeared. Over the years we came to love this particular outspoken lady. She would often say to me, "I 'ate you" (hate) and would give my face a sharp slap. My return was to kiss her on her cheek to which she would say, "You've got a cheek!" It reminded me of some of the scenes in My Fair Lady. On the occasion of her ninetieth birthday Ruth took her a pot of African violets. This meant a climb of thirty flights of stairs, as the lift was broken down, as it often was. She arrived to be greeted by the lady saying, "Wretched, wretched plants; I've got a table full of 'em." (them). Sure enough, she had a dozen or more on the kitchen table. One day she said to me, "I'm not a Christian, Mr. Powell, so there," as if to say, "What do you make of that?" "Well Mrs. -------" I said, "a Christian is someone who has asked Jesus to become the boss of their life." I could have said a lot more. "Oh that," she said, "I did that years ago." Who was I to question this lady's faith that had been her mainstay in life through two world wars and the loss of her husband? There was something about her that was genuine even if expressed in a rather quaint way. Many of the ladies in the group couldn't cope with her. "She is so rude. Mr. Powell ought to tell her to leave," they said but Mr. Powell couldn't do that. In fact I rather enjoyed the banter that grew up over the years. To each one is given a measure of faith and our job is to encourage others into a richer understanding of His love and ways. James talks about having compassion and making a difference to those we minister to.

A good friend of hers made an unexpected call at the house. Ruth answered the door and Mrs. -------, eyeing the spider plant on the window ledge in the hallway said, "Cor love, your plants had babies: all you've got to do is plant their arses in another pot, wait two weeks and then cut the umbilical cord and you've got a whole load more." Nobody in Fraserburgh would have dared say that to Ruth. She was another older person we got to know over the years that followed. They all had a part to play in our lives.

I could have missed life in Fraserburgh terribly but somehow God seemed to block out the past as we focused on the present. Maybe this was helped by a man asking if he could park his twin-hulled boat at the side of the mission. He wanted to rebuild the cabin. So on many occasions I spent time talking to him on the deck, although my thoughts often wandered, imagining Fraserburgh harbour and the seagulls circling overhead.

The children were settled into good schools from our perspective but they had mixed feelings about them. Tina's school had a strong academic emphasis and although she did very well, she wasn't prepared to stay on for 'A' levels, although she took them later in life and finally took her degree after she was married. Cliff was called 'Jock' on his arrival at school. He found it hard to adjust at first but soon did very well. Richard had the furthest to travel as his school was in Southfields.

Ruth and I remember painfully how our three children pleaded with us not to request free school meals but send them to school with packed lunches. We certainly didn't want them embarrassed, so packed lunch it was. The cost of being a preacher's kid is something they had to live with. We tried to make family life fun and as normal as possible, not placing too many restrictions on them. Only they can tell you whether we succeeded. I promised them they would not have to endure any more moves until they decided to leave home. Richard struck up a friendship with a school friend who later became a well-known TV personality. It was he who interviewed Princess Diana when she said, "There are three of us in this marriage." He was often in our house and at times went on holiday to my father's cottage in Wiltshire. One summer he and Richard were on a rugby tour in Wales and for some unknown reason he began to tease Richard and embarrass him saying, "He is a preacher's kid." This apparently went on for several days until one morning when they were walking alongside the swimming pool, Richard decided he had had enough of this and pushed him fully clothed into the pool. Soon Richard was up before the coach who said he was out of order but added in confidence, "Well done, Richard. He deserved it." Boys will be boys.

Ruth's sister Mary and her husband took a real interest in the ministry at the mission. On one occasion she brought with her a talented young lady called Pauline Stubbs. Little did we know at the time what a tremendous help she was going to be in establishing the foundation team of the mission. They arrived one weekend when Ruth was unable to take her Sunday School class so Pauline was asked to take her class. There was an immediate look of embarrassment. She knew that all the children were from the Caribbean. There were no black children in the depths of Sussex and she was overwhelmed at the thought of teaching them. To her credit, she agreed and as a result her life took a dramatic change. At the close of her teaching session, one little child said she would like to pray and ask Jesus into her life. Pauline returned to our house next door full of enthusiasm. "That was the best afternoon ever," she said. Within weeks she was living in Battersea and became part of the family.

"Are you trying to convert me, Ruth?" asked Gaetan as he was handed a Bible at the Filey Bible Week Conference. "I could never do that, Guy," said Ruth, but he took the Bible and made his way into the big marquee to listen to Sidlow Baxter. Whatever happened to him in that meeting we will never know, but it changed his life. He has been a worshipper of Jesus ever since.

During those early days, most of the church came back to our house for Sunday lunch. It was said by many – and Ruth and I know it is true – that the church was formed around our kitchen table. Fortunately we had been able to buy a huge executive table which could easily seat sixteen at a time. We had so much fun as more and more enthusiastic young people joined us. Most of them were first generation Christians and so their parents were very suspicious of us. I believe some parents resented the friendships they were experiencing with us and the family. Ruth and I always encouraged these new believers to keep a good healthy relationship with their parents. Our relationship helped us coin the phrase that was often used in a lot of our publicity, "In the centre of the estate is a family that cares." To this very day the heart of the church is still centred around a 'family table'.

Chapter 10

Weddings

I was totally unaware that Pauline and Gaetan were becoming a little more than good friends. I could hardly believe my ears when one Sunday he took me to one side and said, "When you were in Fraserburgh, I heard that you often took fishermen's funerals." "Well yes, but don't worry, Guy you look pretty healthy. What's the problem?" I replied. Gaetan had a mischievous look in his eye. He was leading me on and I wasn't sure where he was going. "Well, for a change how about trying your hand at weddings?" I still didn't get it, so, with a chuckle he said, "Pauline and I want to get married. Can you help us tie the knot?" That evening we celebrated with them over a fish and chip supper. Their wedding day came round very quickly, and what a day it turned out to be! When I said, "I now pronounce you man and wife," Pauline let out a very loud "Whoopee!!" That was the first of scores of weddings we were involved in over the years to come.

It was always a privilege to officiate at family weddings and my sister's daughter's wedding was a day to be remembered. Rachel and Michael's day was different but equally enjoyable. The entire building was decorated in huge African flowers bought that very morning from Covent Garden. She did not want it to be a conventional ceremony and it certainly wasn't. When the guests arrived at the mission, they were greeted by the bride and groom serving coffee with heart shaped biscuits and strawberries dipped in chocolate. At least that was the idea, but they became so busy talking to the hundreds of guests that Ruth and Jennifer took over the responsibility. Rachel looked stunning in a very unconventional wedding dress. She wore a transparent white lace gown over a black mini shift dress. No white shoes for Rachel either but long black lace-up Doc Marten Boots. She was certainly different, but absolutely radiant and stunning. Michael's suit was likewise unconventional, but together they made a handsome couple. When everyone was present I invited the entire party into the worship area. This was set out in two huge semicircles stretching the entire width of the building. The big issue with Rachel was that she did not want to be the centre of attention and steadfastly refused to walk down a long aisle. She and Michael sat in the circle of chairs with their guests. Her next request was that they didn't want to stand at the front to exchange their wedding vows. So at the given point I walked to them as they sat alongside their close friends, and encouraged by me they stood and quietly exchanged vows. My sister Jennifer sang and spoke and it truly was a special time of celebration. Some people were in tears for reasons only known to the family. The reception and dance were held in the adjoining hall. The food was of the highest quality. Michael, being a chef, saw to that. A friend of theirs dressed in a long black coat entertained with contemporary songs and music. One song will live in my memory for ever. He repeatedly sang the line "Everything is going to be all right." I happened to glance out of the main doors at this time and sadly saw a couple having a punch-up. I didn't want to know who they were, and the singer continued with the reassuring song that, "Everything was going to be all right." And so it was. It was a thoroughly enjoyable day.

One couple introduced candles into the wedding ceremony. Three candles were placed on the communion table. Only the outer candles were lit. At a given point the mothers of the couple came to the front, took the lighted candles and gave them to the bride and groom who in turn lit the centre candle and then blew out the candles they were holding. It symbolised the mothers giving their children to their respective partners and the two becoming one. After a time this became part of several weddings over the years, until one fateful day when a certain mother, on handing the candle to her daughter, failed to see the long lacquered ringlet of hair hanging down from her veil. The flame caught the ringlet which went up in a sheet of flame. There was only one thing I could to do, which was to clap my hands over the flaming hair. Fortunately I put out the fire and the ringlet fell to the ground. Once the drama was over, the bridal party settled down surprisingly well. In my address I could not resist saying that for many years we had longed to see tongues of fire as they did at Pentecost, and now the first time it happened I put them out.

It was my great privilege to officiate at the weddings of all our children. All found their partners in the mission and bought homes in Battersea. Tina and Kevin were the first down the aisle. They went on to have four children. Carol was the oldest and very like her mother. Needless to say she, being the first, became the adoring focus of aunts, uncles and grandparents. She was in a Christmas play at the mission, and I believe she took the role of

Mary. Standing alone and overcome by the congregation's attention, she looked at her mother and said, "I don't know what I am supposed to say." What a darling! Carol was soon followed by the twins, Alexander and Zoe. They were full of life and mischief. We recall a desperate call from Tina: "Mum, come round now: I can't cope with them any more." On her arrival she found Tina on her knees in the hallway attempting to clean up a mess in the shagpile carpet. Whilst she was upstairs they had emptied the entire contents of a pot of marmalade and a box of tea leaves on the carpet. I am told they call these years, 'the terrible twos'. Tina would agree. A few years later Thomas joined the family. He had a glorious head of red hair, which was a special delight to Ruth as red hair ran in her family. They called a halt at four children. The next down the aisle were Clifford and Kym. It was another wonderful wedding with family and friends filling the mission. At first they lived in a small apartment in Queen's Road but moved within a short time into a three-bedroomed house in time for the arrival of Helen, Rachel and Robert. Ruth recalls attending Helen's school play. As far as she was concerned Helen was the star performer, her confident voice standing out above the rest. Rachel loved the little jar of sweets prepared by Ruth when she visited us. Robert, true to family form, loved his football. Clifford worked in Barclays Bank and Kym took a part-time job helping me out with the mission administration. So seven grandchildren arrived in six and a half years.

Richard and Mary were the last to get married and a beautiful wedding took place on the opening weekend of the new mission. Time passed and they settled into their new home in Battersea. Ruth remembers taking them to hospital for the arrival of their first-born. For several hours we waited patiently in a side room. We will never forget the time when the door burst open and Richard announced with pride, "We have a son and his name is Conor." There were hugs all round which included a wonderful friend and midwife called Hannah. Then a year or so later came the arrival of Joshua – the final grandchild and a very handsome one he was. I recall doing a little carpentry in their lovely home with Joshua crawling around the floor trying to get his hands on anything sharp and dangerous. I am pleased to say he didn't succeed. You will understand that our home was bursting at the seams when they all arrived for family celebrations. Great fun, noisy and wonderful days, never to be forgotten. We would love to be able to do it all again if only we could wind the clock back.

Chapter 11

Kids on the Estate

The early days saw us involved in children's work. We were told that seventy per cent of the local school children were from single-parent families. The playschemes financed by the local authority continued throughout our entire time in Battersea. Our small team did a great job. Bible stories, games and more games, outings to Battersea Park, arts and crafts, taking the money at the door, first aid, singing and a great deal of patience and love. The objective of the play scheme was to give the children an enjoyable time in the middle of an ugly estate, while sowing seeds of faith into their young lives.

More than twenty years after our arrival I went into the local dry-cleaning shop and the young assistant said to me, "You remember me, Mr. Powell, don't you? I used to come to your play schemes and clubs, and I want you to know this: they were the best days of my life." We sow and somewhere someone else reaps the harvest.

Kevin was always invaluable when it came to providing music for the children's games. On one occasion, one game required him to play his trumpet and the children had to run around the hall and then freeze when the music stopped. Kevin had totally forgotten about the children and played on and on. He was totally lost in his music. I could see the children were becoming exhausted. "For goodness sake Kevin, stop playing," I shouted above the din of the children. He did, and the children stopped, but in his usual manner he then laughed, and gave a final blast on his trumpet.

Littlehampton was the usual venue for seaside outings. Some children had never seen the sea before and on one occasion they were so excited that they dashed out of the coach and rushed fully clothed into the sea. All this greatly amused the holidaymakers, especially as we had to hang the drenched clothing over the railings in the hope of drying them out by the end of the day. The day ended with seventy damp children back in the coach and the exhausted helpers relieved that everyone was accounted for.

The following year we visited Littlehampton again and at the end of the day one lad was missing, in fact no one had seen him all day. His name was on the list when we left Battersea. The local police were contacted. We toured the town and the beach, which took a long time. I had visions of anxious parents waiting at the centre wondering why the coach was so late in returning home. The usual singing in the coach going home was rather subdued. I stared out of the window. The one hope I had in the back of my mind was that perhaps he had not boarded the coach in the first place. We pulled up outside the mission, and soon parents were reunited with children and to my relief no anxious parent appeared on the scene. When I returned indoors, the phone rang and to my horror the voice said, "This is the Littlehampton police. We have a young lad by the name of ------- and he says he came with you from Battersea, do you know anything about him?" I was just about to say, "Yes, as far as I know one of our children was missing, I'll drive down immediately, and I will be with you as soon as I can," but my reply was cut short by laughter. "It's only me, Tony. Our problems are over, I have just heard that after the child boarded the coach in Battersea he returned home saying he had forgotten his packed lunch. It's okay, Tony. We left Battersea without him." Wow, what a relief! This prank was the work of my good friend Keith who couldn't resist winding me up, although I think I would have done the same to him. Keith was always a tremendous help and support during those early days and shared the vision with me in prayer and practical support.

The children's parents seemed to have no idea that all the helpers were volunteers. With so many children to care for, we had to exercise verbal discipline when it was required. One father took exception to this and I was told he was coming down to 'punch my lights out', whatever that might mean. It certainly was not a friendly visit. He arrived with every intention of sticking to his word. Someone must have been praying for me for he left satisfied with my explanation of our policy.

A weekly Mother and Toddler group was held in the mission, but unfortunately it was not run by a member of the mission. Over the months Ruth got to know the leader and became friendly with the group. As it was held in the mission, she was given a twenty-minute 'God Spot'. This was going well until she asked a local minister to share a few thoughts with the group. He came dressed in a suit and gave them a 'Bible Bashing', whereas what they needed was an interest in their lives and a glimpse of God's love. He needed to learn an important lesson in ministry:- KISS – Keep It Simple Son (or Stupid). One young mum called Tricia had her interest aroused by Ruth's teaching and finally came to faith in Jesus.

Early one Monday morning we were setting up the hall for the annual summer playscheme when a young girl arrived saying she had nothing to do during school holidays and could she be of any help. Looking back we can now see it was one of those divine appointments. She soon made friends with the team and her administrative talents were put to good use. We needed all the help we could get to supervise a hundred noisy children. Kym lived near the mission and for some reason she was under the impression that the six team members were all our children. On the final Friday afternoon she asked, "What happens now?" She was obviously worried what she was going to do with the rest of the summer break. It was an easy answer. "Tomorrow is our day off, Kym, but on Sunday we meet as a church, and if you want to come you are very welcome." And come she did. That morning we had a communion service. Kym was sitting next to Ruth and asked if it would be alright if she took the bread and wine. For two weeks she had not only seen but felt something of God's love for her. She wanted to respond, for all this was new to her. So very quietly Ruth and she prayed together and so started her journey of faith in Jesus. What a tremendous way for her to finish the summer playscheme. That Sunday several people from the church came into our house for dinner. Kym was invited. Before we ate I had a chat with her. I wanted her to be clear about what had happened to her when she prayed with Ruth. "Kym," I said, "you will hear about the Holy Spirit, I want you to know that this morning He has entered your life, He has promised to lead you as you face the future." I then prayed with her. What a privilege! Little did I know that in a few years' time she would be our lovely daughter-in-law. The ministry with children continued for our entire time in Battersea. Thousands must have passed through our doors. We thank God for all our friends who gave of their time and energy to this vital ministry.

Chapter 12

A Voice of Compassion

Directly opposite to our manse stood Atkinson House. It wasn't a single dwelling but a twelve-storey tower block. In the top apartment lived Jean, a young, attractive woman in her late thirties. Ruth happened to strike up a friendship with her when walking back from the local shopping centre. During the course of the conversation, Ruth mentioned the activities in the mission, and Jean quickly volunteered to help Ruth with the handicapped club. She had a warm personality and her help was really appreciated. Ruth enjoyed her company and they soon became friends.

It wasn't long before Ruth discerned that Jean was in need of help herself. This was confirmed when she phoned asking Ruth to visit her in her apartment. She was crying and very drunk. Nothing had prepared Ruth for the shock as she entered the front door. The place smelt of urine and alcohol. It could not be called a home. She was lying half naked on an old couch. Newspapers covered the floor. Ruth sat beside her and held her limp hand. Jean's bloodshot eyes looked at Ruth through a mass of black matted hair covering her face. "Oh no, you poor, poor girl," was all Ruth could say. Jean cried and groaned as she laid her head on Ruth's lap. Ruth tried to make sense of her garbled outpouring, but it was no use talking to her at that time. Jean mumbled words about her partner, how it was all his fault, for he made her drunk. She hated, loathed, detested him.

Right now what she needed was a little tender loving care. Ruth ran a bowl of warm water, found some soap and a flannel and began washing her face, hands and feet, saying as she did so, "We are going to come through this together, Jean."

All this took place to a background of tears and garbled conversation until Jean drifted off to sleep. Ruth then began to tidy the place up. The floor had to be washed and the odd pieces of furniture put into place. She found a piece of expensive porcelain on the mantelpiece and a portfolio full of photographs covering Jean's career. Jean, when sober, spoke with a clear cultured voice, and had enjoyed a lifestyle in the past that bore no resemblance to her present condition. The little porcelain ornament was evidence of her refined taste in those earlier days. When Ruth opened her portfolio, there were countless pictures of Jean dancing in numerous West End shows, and in particular, the Bluebell Theatre shows. She had been an actress and dancer for many years and was also a very accomplished linguist, speaking seven languages.

The hours passed, and after leaving Jean with a cup of coffee in her hand, Ruth returned home telling me of the terrible situation across the road. When sober, Jean was a delight to be with and she continued to help Ruth with the handicapped club. She also came to the mission on a Sunday and Ruth was able to pray with her as she asked

Jesus to become her Saviour. She meant this prayer more than we realised at the time. She confided in Ruth that her so-called partner was a beast in disguise. He treated her abominably and frequently forced her to consume large quantities of alcohol so that he could sexually abuse her. She hated him but couldn't get him out of the house. He was strong and made fun of her newly-found Christian faith. He glared at Ruth whenever they met in the road outside the apartment.

At that time I wore a wooden cross around my neck, as it helped to identify me as a minister in the area. I didn't feel comfortable wearing a dog collar. Jean noticed my cross and pleaded with me to give it to her, something I was more than happy to do, and she found great comfort and security in wearing it. Several weeks passed and apart from an occasional blip she remained sober and came to meetings from time to time and even joined our family around the kitchen table on some Sundays.

We received a phone call during the early hours of the morning. I took the call, and a terrified voice said, "Could Ruth come up and see Jean? She has fallen through the window and is covered in blood. Please help." Ruth overheard the conversation and with a look of horror said, "No, Tony. I can't go. You must fly. Poor, poor Jean. What has happened? I would pass out if I saw the blood, so hurry while I call the ambulance." I threw on a few clothes, crossed the road, and took the smelly lift to the top floor. I found myself face to face with the wretched man. Jean was lying on the floor with a terrible gash from the corner of her mouth to her ear. Broken glass and blood covered her beneath the shattered window. In her drunken state she had fallen and her head had smashed the window. "Do something, for God's sake do something!" He almost screamed this at me. I don't know what he expected me to do. One thing he had done was to call an ambulance and thank God I could hear the siren in the distance. She was far worse than I realised, for her teeth could be seen through the gash. Maybe it was fortunate she was drunk and didn't know what was going on. He looked really scared as the police and ambulance crew took her away.

We later learned the full story that had caused her to fight him off in her drunken state. Her life had been a continual struggle since the beautiful looks that had earned her such praise in the past were gone. We had always been available in friendship and support, but her partner hated us. Her health deteriorated rapidly and her drinking continued. She was fighting a losing battle. Her partner refused to leave the apartment. Some months later we heard the sad news that Jean had died of a massive heart attack. Her body had given up under the constant strain and stress of her life of abuse. We knew we would miss this special person who had become part of our life. As the coffin left her sad apartment, Ruth said, "Thank God she will never be abused again."

Chapter 13

Another God Moment

It must have been around 10.30 one Sunday morning when a police patrol car pulled up outside the mission. A young inspector jumped out and ran towards me with a huge grin on his face. I wondered if he always arrested villains with a smile on his face. Certainly as I was the only person in sight he was obviously after me. Was the pastor about to be arrested by this crazy copper? What had I done? Surely opening the mission doors for a service wasn't a crime? He stopped a few feet from me, smiled and said, "Tony, how fantastic to see you." I then found my nose being pressed against silver buttons on his uniform as he gave me a big hug. "Come on," he said. "It's me, David Austin. Don't you remember me? I was the young cadet at Scotland Yard." I certainly did remember a cadet by that name but that was some time ago. "Well, put me down, and assure residents in the tower block opposite that you are not arresting me," I said. Curtains had been drawn back and faces were appearing. Then I remembered that young fresh-faced cadet who had been seconded to our office. "Let's go into the mission," I said – anything to get out of sight of curious neighbours. "Fancy a cup of tea? We've time before the service," I asked and pushed him through the front doors which hopefully made the point to anyone looking on that I was not being arrested.

Within the time we had together he told me he had never forgotten our conversations in Scotland Yard and that I had helped him to find his faith. He was now a committed Christian and making his way through the ranks in the police service.

A few months later we had another visit from him under rather bizarre circumstances. Clifford and Richard had volunteered to do a sponsored night of bowling and I had agreed to take them. It was to last from 10pm to 6am the following morning. All three of us were a little late in getting ready for the event. I hastily put a meal together as they threw on a few clothes. Ruth had gone to bed early and was asleep. We left the house full of anticipation of an enjoyable time ahead. It so happened that Inspector David Austin was on duty that night and in the course of his duty he paid a security visit to the mission and house. To his surprise, he found the front door of our house open during the early hours of the morning. Switching on his phone he gave a running report back to the station as he entered the house. "I am entering the kitchen and it appears that someone left in a hurry; several drawers are open and clothes are everywhere. This is not normal for this house; it could have been burgled."

He then visited the lounge saying that he was sure the place had been burgled. This was not surprising as we had all left in a hurry, and the boys' clothes were everywhere. As David went up the stairs, Ruth began to rouse from her sleep, and became aware that the voice she could hear was not a dream but reality. Furthermore this 'voice' was making its way to her bedroom and she was alone in the house. She pulled the sheet over her face as the beam of a powerful torch swept the room and shone on her face. Through the bedclothes she could only manage a feeble "Help!" The reply was not what she expected, "It's all right, Ruth, it's only me. It's David." She slowly let the sheet down still terrified. Who on earth was this intruder? What was this David doing in her bedroom? He pointed the torch at his face to reassure her, but this made his presence even more terrifying, as he now looked like a demon from hell. She screamed. David tried to explain who he was, but Ruth was too confused to take it in. Even when he tried to explain why he had entered her bedroom, she disappeared under the sheet in fear. Only Ruth can tell you what her thoughts were at that time, but I am pretty certain they were not pleasant ones. She eventually composed herself and suggested that David made his way downstairs and she would join him in the kitchen. Looking around the mess in the rooms she kept repeating to herself, "How could they do this to me? The place is a tip!" David, of course, agreed with her sentiments and after a cup of tea together in the kitchen left the house with the visit recorded in his notebook. We had a lot of repenting to do when we returned home that morning – and a lot of clearing up!

Chapter 14

Come On, Let's Celebrate

It's amazing how a conversation can change the direction of one's life. It happened that my brother Laurie was staying with us for a weekend and he made the suggestion that I should attend a meeting which was held at the London School of Economics. It was organised by what was then known as the House Church Movement, and the main speakers were Gerald Coates, John Noble, Maurice Smith, Roger Forster and Lynn Green along with a few others. They all appeared to know each other and led significant churches in London. We sat in a large circle. Everyone was on first-name terms. One of the leaders gave a short talk (you were not allowed to call it a sermon). Maurice Smith was sitting near me and he interrupted the preacher saying he had something important to say to the man sitting opposite him. He left his seat, walked across the room and apologised to this man saying he had a wrong attitude toward him and would he forgive him. They had fallen out some time in the past. All this was done in front of everyone. I had never seen anything like this, I was soon to discover this was not unusual among this group of leaders. Soon everyone settled down and enjoyed the evening as though nothing strange had happened. I was impressed, and asked myself, "Who are these people?"

Several further meetings followed and a relationship developed between our mission and Gerald Coates, who lived in Cobham. Little did I know at the time but years ago dad had often picked up Gerald by car in Cobham and invited him and his team to speak at the mission, well before I arrived at Battersea. Gerald was with the Brethren Assembly in Cobham at that time but looking for something different, so he started a small group in his front room that eventually grew into the ministry known as Pioneer. Over the years that followed Gerald and his friend Noel Richards often preached and led worship at the mission. We needed outside input into the life of the mission and everyone looked forward to their visits. We all appreciated their kind support and personal interest in our ministry. On one occasion he asked me to pastor a team going to South Africa. He paid all expenses, which was very good of him. I thoroughly enjoyed the trip. I also admired his preaching. On arrival in Durban, we went straight to a meeting. We were all exhausted but that didn't stop Gerald from standing up front and giving a very inspiring talk. They were a talented group of men and later took prominent positions in the life of the church. Steve Clifford became SEO of the Evangelical Alliance; Noel Richards, an international worship leader and songwriter. They hired Wembley Stadium and Hitler's old stadium in Berlin for huge celebration events. An amazing achievement and tremendous faith.

We started paying regular visits to Cobham for their celebration events. A Bible Week was held at the Leg of Mutton site and we camped at the Boy Scouts' site along with several hundred others. It was great fun and helped create lasting friendships within our fast-growing group of young people. We all have happy memories of Norman Barnes selling 'Barney Burgers' from his BBQ and doing a roaring trade. The next year he sold tracksuits for cold weary campers. Norman was from the East End of London and quite an entrepreneur. Everyone in the church enjoyed his company and I know he had a special regard for us. He had a heart for Africa and he went on to start a charity called Links International. Over the years he raised £1.6 million for needy causes in Africa and around the world. Today he and his wife Grace are still true friends of ours.

Cliff Richard sang at the Bible Week which certainly raised the profile of Gerald's ministry. The preachers were full of the 'new thing' that was happening around the world and we were hungry to hear what was going on. The meetings reminded me of that article I read about the Jesus Movement in California. Now we were experiencing the same thing. One night Gerald invited several leaders including me to join him on the platform. There must have been about twenty of us. I remember Maurice turning round to me and saying with a huge chuckle, "Don't get too excited, brother; you are only in the third row." On reflection I don't think I ever got beyond the 'third row' but that is fine by me.

We camped at various Bible weeks during the course of twenty-seven years in Battersea, culminating in the occasion when we camped with thirty thousand others from Newfrontiers churches at the Stoneleigh Bible Week. Every day was special. We have so many happy memories – late night sessions, steaming hot chocolate in crowded tents, wonderful exaggerated stories, Geoff's warm hospitality and Anne's fun and laughter. I'm sure we kept the neighbouring tents awake. Then during the hot days came the inevitable water fights which were met with a mild rebuke from the platform the following evening.

How could we ever forget the thrilling times of worship, powerful and inspiring preaching? No one could surpass the outstanding preaching of Ern Baxter at the Capel Bible Week. Strong in the Holy Spirit, humorous, an outstanding orator with great intellect, his theme for several years was 'Saul the Head and Shoulders Man: David the Heart Man'. Saul represented the established church with its ecclesiastical pomp and power; David the emerging charismatic church. Bible week followed Bible week. The house church movement grew into many thousands.

Many house church leaders took the platform at Spring Harvest. Mainstream denominations were influenced by their teaching on the gifts of the Holy Spirit. Ministers returned home to their churches taking with them the freedom found in the house churches. Years later came John Wimber with his strong emphasis on 'Signs and Wonders'. Holy Trinity Brompton was his second home when in London. A revived Anglican church emerged and the well-known Alpha course followed soon after. I believe the little group I met with at the London School of Economics had a significant part to play in it all.

Over the years we invited several well-known leaders to preach at the mission. One of them was an Elim pastor called Johnny Barr. This gifted man had a prophetic ministry. We owe him so much. He was from a gypsy family with little or no education. Apparently neither he nor his mother could either read or write until their conversion. He said God taught them to read from the Bible. He was a short man with receding black hair and protruding front teeth. He sometimes stuttered and slurred his words. It is said that the people in the front row got quite a shower. This cockney pastor was someone worth listening to. The deep relationship he enjoyed with God was obvious to all. He wanted to bring everyone into the freedom of life in Jesus that he so much enjoyed. He had a phrase that was mimicked by the young people and that was, "I'll loose you." He often used this phrase when praying with people. Our boys thought he was great. They even called their cat, "Loosya." I told John about this and he really thought it was funny.

He was once invited to preach at the Christian Union in Cambridge University. The meeting was attended by academics. Pictures of the great and noble covered the walls. Never one to be intimidated by others he offered a simple prayer to God, "Lord Jesus, I don't know why you have brought me here, I haven't even got an 'O' level." He believed he heard God saying in reply, "Never mind, son, nor have I." He was quite a character.

After the Sunday service he came back to our house for lunch. During the conversation he said that he had been praying for us and he felt that we should buy our own house. Unless we did so, the mission would never reach its full potential. We were stunned. After he had gone, I said to Ruth, "How on earth do you buy a house with a bank balance of £150? Where do we go from here?" The idea of owning our own home was very appealing but also at the time quite impossible. Or, so we thought.

'Marches for Jesus' took place at this time and our centre was involved in every one. The most memorable was the one that took place in the West End of London. Some sixty thousand highly motivated and enthusiastic believers took to the streets and marched from the north bank of the River Thames, through Westminster then into Hyde Park. Traffic was held up, banners waved, prayers prayed asking God to impact the areas of government, entertainment and commerce. Then came a final rally in Hyde Park and a picnic for the weary marchers.

We decided to launch out and start our own celebration event in Battersea. Scores of churches were contacted and invited to 'Inner City Praise'. We now had a very capable band who led the worship at the mission and a reasonable relationship with a number of leaders involved with the current move of God in and around London. These men readily agreed to come and preach. The brand-new Battersea Leisure Centre was the venue for our celebration. It boasted an impressive hall with bleachers that made comfortable seating for five hundred people. So with a lot of prayer we planned the first event and thank God, hundreds came with a heart to worship and listen. I found it quite exhausting, and the responsibility of planning, arranging, and dealing with the variety of demands left me quite shattered at the end of the day. But of course, it was worth it. There was nothing like it in the area. It was so good to meet up with believers from across the locality. We ran these meetings for three or four years. Battersea was a needy area which presented a great opportunity. We talked this over with the Rev. Sandy Millar who spoke at one of our celebrations, subsequently visiting him in South Kensington. Not long afterwards a team from his church was sent to revive St Mark's, Battersea Rise led by Rev. Paul Perkins.

Chapter 15

New Beginnings

These were really fantastic days, never to be forgotten. At times the number attending our services on Sundays was over one hundred and fifty. We had some capable men in leadership. The oldest was Geoff Hughes, married with four lovely children whose names all began with a 'J'. His fantastic wife, who we came to love so much, was called Anne, of whom more anon. Then there was Colin Collino, at the time a single man. He was a doctor but his heart was in business. He later married Debbie and went on to have three children. Colin eventually left medicine, and being the true entrepreneur that he was, developed numerous businesses. The first enterprise was on the local estate and employed local lads. From there it expanded into a variety of different businesses based both in this and in other countries. Mick Richardson added a great deal to the team. He was a maths teacher, who often led the church in worship. He later married Theresa. They had two boys. Theresa often accompanied Mick when leading worship. They were a true team in ministry and a great blessing to those who had issues requiring wise counsel and prayer. Then finally there was Brian Watts. Like Mick, he was a local – born in Battersea. He was a police sergeant teaching constables at Hendon Police Training College. He was later to marry Jo and have four children. Brian was and still is a very accomplished teacher and leader. Much of what he learned in his career has been helpful to many, not only in Battersea but also elsewhere in the U.K. His wife Jo partnered him in his ministry and she too has encouraged the centre in worship. She is a talented artist and songwriter. Both Brian and Jo are proficient in the martial arts. There was so much talent amongst them all that it was at times quite overwhelming. There were other men in the church who also helped to provide direction for the church. We met every Friday, sometimes in the local pub. I often found it hard to sleep after these meetings where we prayed and thrashed out issues together.

Chapter 16

A House of Our Own

We had not forgotten the prophecy about moving house. Our first option was to approach the local authority for an apartment. Next on the list came the local housing associations. Then of course was the possibility of private rental. All these options were explored, but the authorities refused to help us and private rental was too expensive. In a sense we gave up the quest for alternative accommodation and put the prophecy to the back of our minds. A year later Johnny Barr gave us a mild rebuke, saying, "Unless you are obedient, the ministry will not flourish." We felt trapped. We wanted to move but it seemed impossible. We were desperate. Perhaps Mr. Barr had got it wrong. Geoff Hughes came to the rescue with a plan that was the obvious way forward to him but I didn't like it. He sat us down and said, "There is only one way forward whether you like it or not." He then presented his idea saying, "Over the past years you have ministered into the lives of a considerable number of people. I'm going to write to all these people on your behalf asking them to support you in the purchase of your own house." We did not respond as he expected; for our minds were going into overdrive. The thought of our friends and relations receiving a letter like this seemed so embarrassing to us. Eventually we could see that in spite of our reservations, this was the only way forward. So in due time letters were sent to long-standing friends in the Fishermen's Mission, the hospital, Christian Union and to our family. We could imagine what some would think on receipt of a begging letter, and we wanted to run a mile. However, our leadership team supported this initiative.

Slowly, the funds began to trickle in and to my amazement it reached £7,000. Then the donations dried up. As far as I was concerned that was the end of the idea and I was ready to ask Geoff to send all the money back, kindly thanking everyone for their concern. We had at that time made enquiries about a small end of terrace house with three bedrooms, with a small garden backing onto the busy railway line to Victoria and Waterloo. The asking price was £50,000 but what was the point of making an offer? "No, Geoff, thanks for all your hard work but please send the money back to these kind people." Ruth did not share my attitude. Her reply was, "If my earthly father promised me a bike, he wouldn't give me a front wheel and leave the rest of it in a shop. He would give me the complete bike. Where is your faith Tony?" Of course she was right.

A proposal was made that we should go away for a weekend break, stop worrying, leave it in God's hands and have a good time together. We did have a good time but the surprise that greeted us when we returned outshone the weekend away. Our daughter-in-law Kym met us as we arrived at home. She had a look on her face that said something had happened that was good news. "You won't believe this, but someone has given £10,000!" She knew this because Clifford was the mission treasurer. This was way beyond anything we had ever thought possible. You read about this sort of thing in books but not in a small church in the centre of a large council estate in London. But it was true and was confirmed when we called on Geoff Hughes. So we asked the obvious question: "Who has given us such an amazing amount?" His reply stunned us. "It comes from -------." We stood in his lounge absolutely stunned and speechless. How could this close friend raise this amount of money? No, we could not accept it. How could we accept it? It was incredible. They read our thoughts and before we could say anything they said, "It's in the bank and you cannot refuse it." We were overwhelmed and very humbled that anyone should do such a thing for us. Now the house purchase was possible, as long as a mortgage could be obtained for the balance.

The following weekend confirmed that the way was clear for the purchase of the house. John Noble had arranged some meetings with a young couple from America called Charles and Paula Slagel. This was a Ma and Pa ministry. They sang together, shared their life stories and at times prayed with individuals during the course of the meetings. It was well into the meeting when he pointed at me and asked me to stand saying, "The Lord has a word for you." I had never met this couple before, but the thought of God having a word for me set my heart racing. To my amazement he spoke about my life since I was eighteen years of age, and finished by saying that my monthly income would be increased by £150 and not to worry about the house. What a meeting that was! First a promise of a pay rise and then a command not to worry about the house.

We left the meeting walking on air. That was on the

155

Friday night. The following Monday we had a phone call from Gordon Holloway, the Chief Executive of the Shaftesbury Society, asking us to meet him at head office. He had something important to discuss with us. Yes, we would come immediately. The situation he explained to us was one of urgency. The thirty or so Shaftesbury Centre pastors were urgently in need of a couple to meet with, pray with, encourage and support them on behalf of the society. Gordon said he would like to do this but unfortunately he did not have the time so he was asking us. This would take up two days per week and the Society would pay us £150 a month. I was overjoyed, as firstly it would be a privilege to spend time with pastors and secondly £150 was the amount promised on Friday, only four days ago. This was one of those times in our life that will never be forgotten.

The hymn writer said, "His love in times past forbids me to think he will leave us at last in trouble to sink." Why do I say this? Because when we sold our house prior to going into the Deep Sea Mission it was said by some that we had committed financial suicide, and in many ways I could understand their reasoning. Once you pull out of the housing market, it's very difficult to get back into it, especially when you are over fifty years of age, yet here we were putting down a hefty deposit, with a promised increase in our monthly income of £150 to pay the mortgage. It couldn't be better than that. Within a few months we were happily settled into our new home, Johnny Barr's prophecy had become a reality and the manse was ready for the surgery to move into.

Chapter 17

Disadvantaged and Loved

On one occasion Ruth and I went to hear John Noble preaching at the Anglican church at the Oval, Kennington. His talk was based on the experience of David in the Cave of Adullam. It says in 1 Samuel 22 v 2: "All those who were in distress or in debt or discontented gathered around him, and he became their commander, about four hundred men were with him." We really felt this was a word from the Lord and the mission had to be a 'rescue shop'.

We had used the statement, 'In the heart of the estate is a family that cares,' in our local publicity, and one day, Kevin, one of the young men in the mission, found Stanley sleeping rough on a bench in Battersea Park. We tried to take care of him and found a place for him to sleep in one of our side rooms. In return he swept the floors, locked up and took care of the building at night. He didn't drink or smoke. His stained, ragged clothes were held together with safety pins and string. Most of the time he was clean-shaven. The small part-time job in Harrods sweeping the basement floor paid for his food from the local takeaway. This poor man always carried several heavy bags around with him. I tried to reason with him saying we could lock them away in one of the mission cupboards. He found conversation difficult and any attempt to talk to him was soon curtailed by him saying, "I'm all right, Mr. Powell," and that was that. He did his best to keep fit and did regular exercises in the mission.

He was never any trouble until the day Ruth came home saying, "Tony, run. I'm sure Stanley has hung himself, his body is hanging between the internal doors of the mission. Just go." What on earth was I going to find as I ran the few yards to the mission? Well, he was not trying to end his life. He was doing his routine exercises. He had placed a pole over the two open doors and was doing 'lift ups'. Ruth had unfortunately passed the door when his head was above the door level, and all she could see were two thin white legs protruding from his old grey trousers. So all was well; he just chuckled and left me saying, "I'm all right, Mr. Powell."

One Sunday I was preaching on the 'Army of the Lord', basing my message on Paul's words of 'Fighting the good fight of faith' and developing my theme by saying that at times we were like holy saboteurs and that our faith and action was only seen by God and no one else. The following morning, Stanley was at my door saying, "Mr. Powell, I'm not joining up." I didn't know at the time, but he was an ex-naval man. The poor man had completely misunderstood what I was saying so I said, "That's fine Stanley, just keep on being a door keeper, you're in a different regiment."

Around Christmas time he caught pneumonia. An ambulance rushed him to hospital and there he sadly died. He was a great loss to us all. It was only then that we really began to find out about this loveable character. One very humorous side of our relationship with him was that from time to time he would hand me and others in the mission a slip of paper on which was written a huge sum of money. This he would do in complete secrecy saying, "You'll be all right Mr. Powell, one day you will have enough money for the rest of your life." He would then shuffle off giving a little chuckle to himself. After his death we had to go through his bags to find out who he was and if possible inform his relatives. We soon found some vital information in one of his many bags. First was the address of the Canadian embassy and then of Barclays Bank in Chelsea.

We had an interesting time with the manager of Barclays Bank. I phoned asking if they knew Stanley and to my utter surprise they said, "Yes." My immediate thought was that he really did have money stashed away. The manager went on to tell how Stanley came into the bank on regular occasions and would hand the cashier a slip of paper on which was written a figure of several thousand pounds saying, "Pay this into my account." The trouble was that there was no money to accompany the slip of paper. The cashier got to know Stanley pretty well and went along with his delusion, however, my hope of riches quickly evaporated. Stanley was penniless.

He kept several hundred carefully-written exercise books in tea chests under the stage. In these books were plans of how he would defend England if attacked by the Russians. Each book commenced by saying he was 'King Stanley of Great Britain' followed with pages of detailed military tactics. It was very repetitive, and complete nonsense.

Next we contacted the Canadian embassy. To our surprise we learned he was known to them too. Apparently he was a commissioned officer in the Canadian Navy during the second world war. His ship was torpedoed on a run to the U.K. This seriously affected his mental stability. He was offered a retirement rest home for the rest of his days, but he refused. His father had come across to England on several occasions looking for him but without success. The embassy knew he was in London as Stanley called on them from time to time. Without my asking, the embassy said they would pay for all funeral expenses and a senior representative would attend the funeral. The funeral service was held in the mission and afterwards we invited everyone into our house for refreshments. I then asked the representative to speak about Stanley. He related his story and finally said, "No; Stanley died penniless," and, "He lived most of his life in mental confusion." The embassy gave me the address of his father in Canada and I was able to write to him saying that in a small way we were able to give a little support during his last years. His reply was one of heartfelt thanks. We all missed Stanley. All that was left was the task of burning three tea chests full of his writings on national security. Richard, my son, did this, and it was a very emotional business as this was Stanley's life work. It became a 'Holy Bonfire'.

Over the years several other disadvantaged people came to the mission. One of them was Rose. She, like Stanley, had lived rough until the Catholic church gave her accommodation in Westminster. She would often come to the house for a chat. Her great delight was to watch Ruth doing the family ironing in the kitchen. It reminded her of her childhood days. She often came to the evening service and would regularly leave halfway through for a cigarette. She used to wink at me as she left as if saying, "You understand, don't you?" I think I did.

We also got to know a young Scotsman appropriately called Jock. Unlike Stanley he was a very heavy drinker. His visits to us were irregular. All he wanted was a place to sleep. He once urinated into a chest holding Stanley's exercise books. If I remember rightly Jennifer, my sister, sorted that problem out.

From time to time some of the elderly ladies from the residential home next door came to the services. On one occasion one of them stood up during the sermon, turned around on the spot several times and said in a loud voice, "Goodnight, everyone. Happy Christmas," and promptly walked out. This was in the middle of summer. The preacher on that occasion was Maurice Smith. He went home saying, "I've never been wished a Happy Christmas in the middle of summer!"

My mother used to say, "Some people have weak machines to drive," and I believe that was true of Stanley, Jock and Rose and a few others I could mention, including Mrs. C who used to slap me round the face for a bit of fun. It was our place to offer them a little love in their broken and sad world. I wish we could have done more.

Chapter 18

Ships That Pass in the Night

The St Thomas' Hospital Christian Union needed houseparents for their weekend house party. Theresa Richardson, a member of both the Christian Union and the mission asked if we could help out. We happily agreed and thoroughly enjoyed being with this fun-loving, energetic bunch of medics, physios and nurses. The committee said, "It's possible you will never meet with most of us again; we are like ships that pass in the night. Each year we have different houseparents." That certainly was not the case as our relationship with this special group lasted for several years. On the first weekend away the speaker found the responsibility too much and waffled his way through the first session. As he preached, I put my finger under a sentence in the Bible where it said, "When the Spirit moves," doing this for Ruth's sake. However, the young Colin Collino who was sitting behind saw my silent protest and took heart, realising he was not alone in his reaction to the gentleman up front. After the meeting, the preacher told us he had developed a headache and would not be able to stay for the next two sessions. To be honest, I think most of the students were pleased to see him packing his bags.

On every other occasion, the sessions were just brilliant

and we formed lasting relationships with a growing number of students. Among them were David Finch, Colin Collino, Paul Burgess and many others. As time went by, they all qualified as doctors and moved out of London. Like the proverbial 'ships' we never expected to see them again. Although out of sight they were not forgotten, and here the story takes a dramatic turn.

One Monday morning Ruth was standing at the sink reflecting on the good times with the Christian Union at St Thomas' Hospital. Her thoughts turned to a brief prayer for the doctors. Suddenly she felt a strong desire to contact David Finch and tell him he should leave his current post of GP and start a practice in our manse next door to the mission. This was rather a radical idea for we knew he was now well settled in his new practice, living in a nice location in Portsmouth and enjoying sailing his yacht in the Solent. Why should he want to come to Battersea and open a surgery in the centre of a rather miserable council estate? She finished the washing-up and got on with the day's chores. A short time later the doorbell rang, and there standing on the doorstep was David Finch. With a little gasp she said, "David, come in, I can't believe it; what are you doing here?" He stood in the centre of our living room and explained to Ruth that he had been driving up to London on medical business when he felt a tremendous urge to call at our house. What he was really saying was, "What have you got to tell me?" Ruth's reply was, "David, I don't think you will want to know," and she really did not want to let him know. "Come on, tell me," he said. "Well, it's simply this. I feel the Lord is telling me to tell you that you should start a surgery in our manse in Battersea." Hearing this, he fell back onto the sofa behind him. Poor David; this must have been an awful shock to him or was it? Was he not half expecting some direction for his future? At the time we did not know that he and several friends were wanting to work together in a general practice.

After a strong coffee and catching up with family news he left the house, shaken, and realising that his call at the house was more than an interesting coincidence. What was he going to do with this revelation? Was this God's answer to their prayers? For us it appeared to be the way ahead. We had moved out of the manse as directed in the prophecy given by Johnny Barr. Surely this was the reason for it. Where should we go from here? The most important question was "Is God in this?" If the answer was "Yes," then all would be well, no matter what difficulties lay ahead. What ensued was a wonderful experience of seeing everything fall into place and a vision become reality. Within a short time things began to happen, starting when an elderly doctor visited us asking for advice. She said that she would be retiring in a short time and did we know of a nice young doctor who would take over her practice? She knew of our connection with St Thomas' Hospital and thought we might know of someone to take over. Now perhaps as you read this you are saying, "Life is not that straightforward; come on, Tony; there must have been more to it than that." The answer is that it really did happen like that and furthermore this call was followed by another elderly doctor on the estate retiring from her practice. It was amazing.

All this information was relayed back to David. He and others by this time were going down the official route in the medical world and all we could do was to look on and support them in prayer and help in any practical way. In area after area a firm "No" was in time turned into a very positive "Yes." Finances, moving house, schools and a hundred and one other details were dealt with. All this was accompanied by a lot of excitement and prayer. Slowly, slowly, everything began to fall into place.

The mission building was proving to be too small to accommodate the growing numbers and daily activities. With the proposed sale of the mission house to the doctors and subsequent release of money, the Shaftesbury Society Council were asked if we could increase the size of our buildings. To this they kindly agreed and promised to help with the finance. We proposed a new hall seating three hundred, three apartments for staff or friends of the mission, conference rooms and offices, and a new kitchen. All this was agreed and contracts were drawn up and accepted. Needless to say this generated a huge buzz, both for the proposed surgery and also the new mission facilities. Everyone was behind the project and prepared to give in order to make it possible. A Sunday was set for everyone to give sacrificially to meet the cost. Walking to the mission I said to Ruth that my hope for the offering would be in the region of £11,000. My estimate didn't seem to impress her. She had been in conversation with one of the doctors and together they felt that if God was in it then the offering would be more than £20,000. I thought that such an amount would be fantastic. Our fellowship responded in a way that was far beyond anyone's wildest dreams and at the close of the service, Clifford, who was the treasurer at that time, made an announcement to say that the amount given in the plastic bucket up front came to the staggering amount of £40,000. For the next nine months the building and house were torn apart and out of the scaffolding and building site emerged our fantastic facilities.

The opening of the mission was a grand occasion attended by the Earl of Shaftesbury, the Mayor, a local member of Parliament and the Shaftesbury Council members. Gordon Holloway, the General Secretary, was one hundred per cent behind the project. We all owe a lot to him. Many hundreds of past and present friends associated with the mission also came. It was a great evening and we opened without any debt whatsoever.

The following Sunday was even better. By a very happy coincidence it was the wedding of Richard and Mary. It was a wonderful day for them. Ruth and I could not be happier to see her standing at Richard's side. They were so right for each other, and are both loved by us and many others. During the celebration, I looked back to the time when answering the phone in the kitchen, I heard this Irish voice asking about the time of the Sunday morning service and whether it would be alright to attend. And of course she came. Her visit was another of those 'God moments' both for us and for her. The wedding was most enjoyable with many of her family coming over from Ireland. It was 'top hat and tails' with the ladies in their very best. The reception was held in an outstanding restaurant in the West End. It was a true celebration with a lot of fun and goodwill.

Not long after this, the day finally arrived for the practice to open and a dedicated team walked into the brand-new premises. They faced quite a challenge to make the practice work. Ruth remembers the day so well. Dr David Finch and Dr Julian Churcher were the GPs. She and Janice were the receptionists while Debbie Collino, Colin's wife, who was also a qualified nurse, became the practice manager. They were a great team and full of faith. Ruth recalls the time when the first one hundred patients were registered and how a little cheer went up from them all. In the early days, all the team would meet with us on Sundays and together we prayed with faith for the success of the surgery and the mission. The members of the mission welcomed the surgery and many joined the practice. Over the years Ruth and I met with the staff every week for prayer and friendship, and shared a joint vision for the area. What impact would the surgery make? Only time would tell.

An old friend of mine once said to me, "Constant change is here to stay." How true that is, for in the course of time fresh opportunities opened up for the surgery and the mission. The initial need to depend on each other was no longer required. It was a painful time, for relationships were tested but the friendships remained. Looking back it is amazing how a chance remark made by Theresa in the St Thomas' CU would lead to a General Practice being established on the Doddington Estate in Battersea. Certainly, God moves in a mysterious way.

Chapter 19

A Catalogue of Disasters

I had been chatting to Richard about the difficult days in the seventies and eighties. There is no doubt about it that his memories of those times were very clear and had made a lasting impression on him. Life could be pretty raw on the council estate reputed to be one of the worst in London. "Dad do you remember the guy who fell to his death from the tenth floor?" he said. "Then there was the little girl who was murdered in the basement opposite our house, and the night the guy smashed his car through the garage doors?" Of course I had not forgotten. How could I?

On most weekends there were heavy drinking parties going on in the tower blocks that surrounded our manse and the mission. During the early hours of the morning one young man decided to accept the ultimate challenge of daredevilry. With his mates cheering him on he climbed out of the window, lowered himself over the edge, and holding onto the window ledge he attempted three pull-ups. This was a regular stunt at these so-called parties but this time it ended in tragedy. His strength gave out and the poor young man fell to his death. What a terrible waste of life.

Then there was the terrible murder of a little girl in the basement of the tower block opposite us. Of course we knew the family and gladly offered our support, but what is that in the face of such a vile and wicked act? The police were constantly at our door and the whole incident was something I would rather forget.

The constant noise of fire engines' bells, police sirens, the smell of lifts used as urinals, the sight of damaged property and graffiti along with the parties that went on till the early morning. In such circumstances it was not surprising that nearly everyone on the estate was on the local authority transfer list. The general attitude was, "Get me out of here." A close relation once said when visiting us, "Darling, I wouldn't live here even if you paid me." Yet we knew this was where we should be and in many ways Ruth and I had been prepared for this over the years – or maybe I should say I was, and Ruth, with amazing grace, came along with me.

Our three children were wonderful throughout it all. There was one incident when one of our children was somewhat overcome with the trouble on the estate and took refuge in our bed. "Mum," he said, "this is awful, and my stomach is in knots." Ruth put her hand out to comfort him, "Oh my," she said, "you are in a bad way, your tummy really is knotted up." She never forgot his reply: "Mum, that's my back not my stomach." They both had a good laugh, maybe the best way to overcome fear.

As for the smashed garage door, again this was another tragic event that I would rather forget. However, it provides an insight into our life in Battersea and needs to be told.

The mission was visited by a young man who had come from a very troubled background. He was lonely and looking for friendship and acceptance. I remember him saying that he wanted to be "part of our lot and how did he join?" We had a positive conversation, prayed together and I hoped the mission life would help him. At first he appeared to be getting on well with everyone but after some months his relationship with some of them went seriously wrong, although I had no idea at the time. All this sadly became too much for him and affected his mental balance. Everything came to a head during the early hours of the morning. Just after midnight our family and neighbours were woken by the sound of a car being driven up and down the road at tremendous speed and the driver shouting abuse in our direction. To our horror we soon discovered it was our young friend. Not only was he shouting abuse but he was also waving an evil-looking machete out of the window, and threatening to attack a couple living in the mission apartment next door. "I'm coming to get you," he shouted, naming our friends. To go out and reason with him was out of the question. He was out of control and soon the tower block windows were full of faces watching the drama. He was determined to attack them. Between him and the young couple's apartment were two heavy 6' garage doors. Suddenly he swung the car around and at full speed smashed through them, wrecking the doors and his car. I immediately phoned the police. Fortunately they came before he could do any further damage to himself or the couple in the apartment. He was arrested and taken to Battersea police station. Shortly afterwards a very shaken young couple emerged from the apartment grateful for the prompt arrival of the police. They didn't press any charges. After a few weeks in prison he returned to the mission full of apologies. Needless to say it took a long time before he came to terms with the issues that had caused him to rebel in such a violent way. However, like so many in life, it took a lot of patience, prayer and loving support and his acceptance of the grace of God before he made it. He is now a well-adjusted man and the last time I saw him he was running a home for disadvantaged youngsters.

The Saturday night parties usually kept us awake till the early hours of the morning, so at the Sunday morning service those who knew about the problem enquired as to how we slept that night. On some nights we hardly slept a wink. Kevin, a young man in the congregation, took the situation into his own hands, and grabbing his trumpet, he went to the offending apartment, pushed open the letter box and blew his trumpet with the full force of his lungs to wake the occupants. The door was slowly opened by a bewildered elderly lady, but before she said anything, Kevin exploded in anger saying, "I have come from the church opposite. The pastor and his family have not slept a wink all night. For goodness stop this terrible racket every weekend." Her reply is worth while repeating: "We are Christians here too, you know, so clear off." It was an interesting reply but before Kevin could say anything else several angry men began making their way to the door and they certainly didn't appear to be 'Christian'. For all Kevin's efforts the parties continued. In time, however, the local authority managed to stamp out the night-long parties with threats of eviction and fines.

Richard went on to remind me of the time we woke one morning to the chanting of "Jesus Christ murderer, Jesus Christ murderer." Looking out of our bedroom window we saw several young black men sitting on the 6' brick wall that surrounded our garden and house. For some reason they did not like us. It felt eerie, evil and very threatening. We could have rung the police but decided not to, in the hope that they would go away. For some unknown reason they suddenly stopped chanting, slid off the wall and disappeared into the walkways surrounding our house. I had no idea what was going on and we never found out.

Chapter 20

Youth Work with a Difference

Our young people decided to mark the opening of a youth club with a concert. Flyers were delivered all over the estate. It was a free concert so needless to say many people came, packing out the hall. The vast majority of these children were somewhat boisterous, to say the least. Sky Rider was first on; the music was great and the songs carried a Christian message. Lights in the hall were dimmed and the stage lights came on. Everything was going well. Colin had purchased a couple of red navigational flares for effect. The result was fantastic, except that the flares produced a choking red dust that smothered everyone present, so doors were hastily opened to clear the air. Nonetheless Sky Rider was a hit, smoke and all – no doubt about that. The crowd loved the band and even the red dust. A short talk then followed and the kids were told about the proposed youth club at the mission. Free food and drinks followed.

Then it was the turn of Rev Counter and the Speedos. Unknown to the leaders, word had been passed around the room to invade the stage when the second band came on. The first few songs were greeted with a mixture of boos and cheers and then it was mayhem. All one hundred kids surged towards the stage. Several then jumped onto the stage and danced about. The lead singer did his best to carry on but the Battersea lads wanted to sing their songs instead. The band had to stop playing. Fortunately the kids did not turn nasty and having made the point they soon left the stage. Richard tells me that nobody was hurt except the feelings of these young musicians from the leafy suburbs. They had never witnessed anything like this before. Order was finally restored and not to be beaten, The Speedos finished the concert. This was very brave and good of them, for they could have walked out after the disturbance. We wondered afterwards whether maybe they had been only too happy to leave Battersea behind. Life is an interesting learning curve. Nothing attempted, nothing gained. Although the evening was a success, the proposed club wasn't. Young Afro-Caribbean lads turned up in gangs and the whole event soon became impossible to manage. The smoking and drug taking forced us to close it down. In time the police would have done the same. If we had had an army of helpers, great things could have been accomplished but sadly 'the labourers were few'. It was about this time that my Ford Capri was stolen from outside the mission. I did eventually get it back. It was found wedged between two lamp posts on a nearby estate. The engine was fine but both front wheels finished up by the doors. I really loved the sleek lines of that car and its real sporty look.

One very hot summer the riots in Brixton and Clapham Junction spilled on to our estate. It was an awful time to be living on the Doddington estate. The atmosphere was electric – law and order disappeared. Gangs of young men invaded the Co-op store filling their trolley then walking out giving two fingers to the cashiers. Nobody dared stop them. It was chaos. Ruth happened to be in the shop at the time and saw one of the youngsters we had known in the mission. She bravely challenged him saying, "Peter, you should know better." He tried to hide his face saying, "It's not me, Miss." He was a youngster we had grown to like over the years but now in the company of his mates he couldn't resist the opportunity of free food and alcohol. The situation got worse as gangs of youths from nearby estates joined in the fray. It became outright battle between the police and black youths. They took up their position on uncovered walkways and armed themselves with petrol bombs. The police massed outside our house, truncheons were drawn, shields raised and they fought back. Bottles were hurled from the balconies followed by bricks and stones, this lasted several hours. An outstanding Christian leader from Providence House in Clapham Junction tried to stop some of his youth club being arrested and finished up with them in jail for the night. After a few days it all calmed down.

During our time in Battersea, glue sniffing emerged as a popular activity among several teenagers. Mick and Theresa, members of the mission, had a real heart for the kids. Several times a week they invited them home trusting that the love and attention given to them would help them break the habit. These kids had little or no support at home, and they appreciated the friendship shown to them. One day Mick and Theresa were surprised to see them at their front door clutching a beautiful bunch of flowers. Needless to say they showed their surprise and of course thanked them. The reply was not what they expected, "It's no trouble; there are plenty more in Battersea Park." Sadly three of the group died through sniffing glue.

These incidents are typical of violence and crime which characterised the area, and sadly, very few had a happy ending, but that is life. We cannot as Christians expect to change everybody everywhere, but we can change someone somewhere. All we are called to be is 'faithful'. Our mission statement was 'In the middle of the estate is a family that cares'. We tried to do this.

Chapter 21

Divine Appointments

The monthly fraternal at the Shaftesbury Society was a great opportunity to keep in contact with its thirty pastors in London. We all needed the encouragement given by the General Secretary Gordon Holloway and the ministry of leaders like Roger Forster. At one of these meetings we heard about the work of the Prison Fellowship and I began to feel this was something I could get involved in. I already knew that the Battersea Methodist minister was the Free Church chaplain at Wandsworth Prison. He had often spoken to me about it. After one meeting I went to see him asking if I could be of any assistance. To my amazement he said that next month they were holding a week's mission and I would be welcome to join the team. The leader of the team was to be Rev. David Watson. Not really knowing what to expect I presented myself at the prison chaplain's office on Monday morning. I imagined that I would be part of the team sitting in the prison chapel listening to David. We were then told that David was not well enough to lead the week's mission and the event was down to us. I believe there were about six of us on the team. The Church Army officer David Kearns led in prayer and then told us we would be taken individually to our various meetings by a prison officer. At this stage I was beginning to wonder if I would be able to meet the challenge. Prison officers soon appeared and each of us was marched along the balconies wondering what lay ahead. I imagined visiting individual cells, sitting with prisoners on bunk beds, and sharing my faith on a one-to-one basis. My illusions were soon shattered as I was led into a room containing thirty men all sitting around the wall looking pretty bored. The prison officer then said to me, "Okay, Sir; this is your lot. I'll be back in one hour; best of luck." He then left the room and locked me in. I groaned within. "Where do I go from here?" I thought of the days in the Deep Sea Mission in Lowestoft, dishing out hymn books to half drunk fishermen. "That's the answer," I thought, "I will start with a few songs to break the awful silence." I realised there was no piano and certainly no evidence of hymn books. On these occasions I usually say or shout a brief prayer, "Help!" At least I think I did. I just had to wing it. As far as I remember, I shared some experiences of life among the fishermen in Scotland. Always a good fallback on such occasions. Fortunately the men were kind and listened to my stories. I began to relax and the laughter coming from them made the hour soon disappear. Some took the opportunity to chat quietly with their friends. I could hardly say, "Come on lads, settle down." These men were often banged up in their cells for twenty-three hours each day. The one thing I didn't mention was my time in the Metropolitan Police, for I wanted to leave the cell in one piece! Nonetheless in some strange way I felt at home in their company. It turned out to be a great week, especially when several men asked for prayer. It was a joy to minister to them.

I found a real friend in David the Church Army officer. He invited me back to speak at the midweek Chaplain's hour. This became a monthly booking that lasted for twenty years. Each time I took with me a small team and each member came prepared to share if asked. We always enjoyed the time with these men. The team included my sister Jennifer who could sing and play the piano. It was also great to have Ann Hughes, Doug and Willy Miles and Warwick Murphy on the team. We usually left the last ten minutes open for feedback from the men. They would often ask for prayer. Over the years several found a living relationship with Jesus as Lord and Saviour. They just loved to sing hymns. It was my practice to ask them if they could remember when they first heard the particular hymn we were singing. Many prisoners were from overseas and referred back to mission schools they attended in Africa or told us that their mothers used to sing hymns around the home.

From time to time we took in a drama team and then the attendance rose from fifteen to one hundred plus. One week we were in the main chapel doing a drama presentation. One of the props was a breadknife. Somehow it was left on the communion table for all to see. I watched as one of the prisoners walked to the table and picked it up. He felt the blade and walked towards me. My mind just raced away, "Oh no! This is it! Nobody else has seen him: whose crazy idea was it to bring it in?" He then turned the blade around and handing me the handle said, "We are not all honest men in here, mate; I think you had better look after this." I shall never forget his words. It took time for my heart to resume its natural beat. On another occasion there was an emergency and a complete prison lockdown and we were unable to leave the chapel for several hours.

We always left these meetings believing that in some small way we had been able to offer friendship in the name of Jesus. A few of the prisoners made their way to the mission on their release; it was great to see them. One of them eventually became an Anglican curate at St Mark's, Battersea Rise. The privilege of ministering to these men came to a close after twenty years. The final service was an emotional time. It's not too often you get hugged by prisoners. Looking back, I am so pleased I visited the local chaplain and offered my help. Mind you in all that time, I never told the men that I used to be a 'copper'.

Chapter 22

It's Time to Seek the Lord

Not far from Battersea are the huge open spaces of Richmond Park. This was to become my 'prophet's chamber'. I set aside a week of prayer and fasting. The weather was great and I could sit in comfort under the old oak trees reading, praying and sometimes sleeping. The only sustenance I took was hot orange and honey twice a day. After three days the hunger left me. Ruth gave me some strange looks, for she knew how much I enjoyed my food. It was not my intention to prepare sermons but just to be alone and talk things over with God. Nothing would please me more than to tell you that I had a vision or special visitations but nothing outstanding happened. The park was a great place to be; the deer were a delight to watch, as were the ducks around the ponds. Dad used to fish in these ponds when he was a boy. He told me on one occasion he caught several fish and put them in his 'keep safe net' tied to his ankle. If caught by the park keeper, he would have to return them. He wanted to take them home as a prize catch. My week was a profitable time and passed very quickly.

Saturday arrived and I began preparations for the morning service. Unfortunately, the week of prayer didn't produce a sermon, and I was tempted to think it had been a wasted time in the park. The evening arrived with still no inspired thoughts for the meeting, so I prayed my emergency prayer, "Help." Sunday morning came, and I was up bright and early ready for the inspired word to fill my mind. Nothing. Once again, "Please Lord, at least some inkling of an idea." Nothing. Finally, jotting down a couple of random thoughts, I made my way to the mission.

To be honest everything seemed the same – a good crowd was present, the worship went as normal, but then something changed: my so-called 'random thoughts' became alive with meaning. I closed my eyes to concentrate on what I was saying. I don't know for how long, but maybe a few seconds. When I opened them I found a young woman called Suna from Turkey standing beside me. The fellowship had watched her leave her seat and stand next to me. This had never happened in the mission before. I wondered what I should say to her, but we both needed time. I turned to her and asked, "Can I help?" A quiet voice said, "Yes, I want to give my life to God." That was not the reply I expected. "Can we pray together?" I asked. "Yes. I would like that." This truly was a 'God moment'. We prayed together. She simply handed her life over to God. The effect on the congregation was electric. Within a short time she was joined by several others all intent on 'giving themselves to God'. Suna was from a church in North London. On her return to her church she started a group for single parents. A few years later she returned as a missionary in Turkey.

Charles and Paula Slagel were with us for a ministry weekend at the mission. The Saturday night meeting was full of people, many wanting personal prayer or a word of prophecy. Some left with a fresh understanding of God's will in their lives. Others were disappointed that nothing was said to them, and felt overlooked. This is always the down side of such a meeting. Sunday morning came and as expected, Charles and Paula led the service. However, to everyone's surprise Charles said, "I'm sorry but I am not going to preach this morning." Now when you are a leader this sort of situation is challenging, to say the least. "What do we do next?" I thought. However, he quickly added, "I believe Ruth has something to say to us." I don't know how everyone reacted to that, but I felt relieved. Although surprised, Ruth had been prepared for this situation. I had better explain.

She cared for a lot of people. Their burdens became her burdens and she was without doubt a tremendous help to people in need. There came a time when it became too much for her. Her anxiety increased when so-called friends began to criticise her and say things like, "You are a typical minister's wife," and, "Come on, get a life; don't get so involved." This hurt her a great deal and she broke down feeling betrayed by those who didn't understand her heart. I found it devastating to see her crumple in this way. This was serious – Ruth was having a breakdown and needed medical help. This was not the Ruth that I knew. We both had to take time out. A little treat seemed the right thing and we found a hotel where we could relax and hopefully return to normality, but it didn't seem to work. That night I phoned my brother Laurie and told him the sad tale. His response came as quite a shock: "Tony, just believe in yourself." I realised I also need help; I had never experienced a breakdown before. But he was right; I had to keep calm and believe it would pass.

That night Ruth had a vivid dream. Jesus picked her up, placed her on his shoulders and walked her around our council estate. This meant so much for her. As a child she used to love to sit on her father's broad shoulders and go for walks beside the sea. The feeling of being carried above everything on strong shoulders was what she needed, and in the dream she heard Jesus saying, "The church is my responsibility not yours; this estate is my responsibility not yours." She woke and her smile said it all. Here was the answer. God had spoken: time would heal. This dream was followed by another that made her laugh in her sleep. I could only watch and chuckle at the obvious joy she was experiencing. She deserved it. Several weeks later in a special meeting God reminded her again that He was in control of the church and the same sense of His presence filled her with relief and laughter.

So when Charles said, "Ruth, you have a word for the church," she immediately walked to the front and said, "All I know is that the Lord would want you to know that He is in charge, not you." She invited anyone who so wished to come to the front to receive prayer. Two or three came forward, as she started to pray for each person, they burst into laughter and collapsed on the floor. The same thing happened to the second and the third. Ruth could not contain herself and started laughing herself. By this time, the queue was stretching down the aisle. 'God's party time' had taken over the meeting. Charles continued to play at the keyboard, thrilled, I believe, to see a church that had served the community so well enjoying a big "Thank You" from their Heavenly Father. I believe it was "Well done, good and faithful servants." As is well known this phenomenon was repeated all over the country in hundreds of churches and was called the Toronto Blessing. One or two folk didn't understand what was going on and we didn't see them again, but they had never felt the strain of carrying the cross that Jesus spoke about, and didn't understand that He was giving us a season of joy.

Several months later, I was in a huge church in North London listening to Charles preach. He came to the end of his sermon and spoke publicly to me. "I have a word for you, Tony." My heart raced at the thought of God having a word for me. I was keen to listen. Maybe it would be a word of encouragement so I obediently stood. All the congregation listened. The word was short and puzzling. "Tony, you will have a ministry among leaders and presidents of nations." "Charles," I thought, "you have asked the wrong person to stand; you have definitely got your wires crossed." My mind went into overdrive, and I had the ridiculous thought of going to 10 Downing Street and chatting to the Prime Minister. All this lasted about ten seconds. I decided it was total nonsense, and the best thing was to forget it and get on with life. Or was it nonsense?

Ten years passed and the word became reality. Thanks to a good friend of mine called Howard Tingley I found myself included in a party of politicians from the House of Commons who were visiting the Balkans. They were a 'Peace and Reconciliation' group and I was the 'Minister' of the party. We visited Macedonia, Albania and Serbia. In each country we spent time with senior politicians. I was invited to close each session with prayer.

A meeting had been arranged with a senior politician

in Albania. After passing through endless corridors and armed guards we found ourselves in his huge office. We introduced ourselves while coffee was served and then settled down in comfortable lounge chairs. This man had a picture of Mother Teresa on the wall behind his desk. Howard had met him before and he seemed genuinely pleased to see us. He smiled when Howard mentioned politicians known to him in London. They had sent greetings from the 'Peace and Reconciliation' group. He spoke about the pressure of political and family life for several minutes and his relationship with those he had met in the House of Commons. The conversation came to an end and Howard suggested I closed the time in prayer. Because he appeared so friendly I asked if I could read a scripture. A nod from him was sufficient. I read the story of Jesus washing the feet of the disciples. I added that Jesus was the finest leader known to man and that leaders of any political party could learn from His example. Humility was not weakness but strength. Our meeting came to a close, we shook hands and left the room. As we retraced our steps along the cold corridors of power, Howard said to me, "Did I see tears in his eyes as we left the room, Tony?" Something registered, I thought, but only God knows. Politicians need our prayers. This man carried huge responsibilities. I don't know what was going on in his life, but God did.

We were sitting in the hotel lounge in Macedonia drinking coffee waiting for a young politician to join us. Howard had met him on his previous visits to the country. He arrived on time and greeted us with hugs and smiles. He spoke about his wife and family, and the hopes he had for his party. Most of the conversation was way over my head.

It's not easy to understand the political life in the Balkans. He had been caught up in the deadly struggles between neighbouring countries. His ambition was to become vice-president. Time came to finish the conversation and once again I was asked to pray. Prior to visiting the Balkans I had been reading the experiences of Daniel's political involvement in Babylon and his relationship with God. Seeing our friend's name was Daniel, or Dan, as he preferred to be called, I had a feeling that this word might be for him. So I briefly shared a couple of thoughts and prayed for him and his family. In the middle of the prayer I had this vivid picture of him as a boy kneeling at his bedside. After praying, I asked if I could share my picture with him. I then described an old double bed with a wrought-iron bedstead and a highly coloured quilt. He was kneeling beside it in prayer. I finished the story by saying, "Dan, I think He is saying He misses you." He stood up and walked to the window and stood staring out into the road for several minutes. You could sense he was trying to compose himself. We waited in silence, with Howard looking at me wondering what was going on. Was this to be the end of a good friendship? After a time he turned and walked across the lounge. Dan had tears in his eyes. "You are so right – the quilt, the bedstead, me praying." He was finding it difficult to get the words out. I believe he was hearing the call of God saying, "I have missed you." He was lost for words and sat back in his chair. After a time he said, "I think I should go home now," and quietly left. On his arrival at home he shared the story with his wife. They sat on the bed together and read the first three chapters of Daniel, recognising that God was speaking to them. At two in the morning they prayed to a Father God who had plainly said, "I miss you."

Life for them would never be the same again.

Some time later I met his mother who confirmed the picture. She could remember him as a little boy kneeling at his bed complete with quilt and iron bedstead. She then said to me, "You know that his father was a pastor, don't you?" Of course we had no idea. Dan told me a year later that the 'encounter' had changed his life forever. I often wonder what he is doing now.

We finally came to the end of our series of meetings in Albania. The team had been led by a member of the British Government, a politician from Norway, an academic from Scotland, Howard and myself. We had been invited to a farewell lunch in a smart hotel. We sat facing our hosts across a long table. Towards the end of the meal the leader of our party left the centre seat came to me and said, "The government officials have asked if you would talk to them about prayer." My response to him was, "Are you sure? Is that true?" I replied, "Give me a couple of minutes and I will exchange seats with you." Then I prayed one of my shorter prayers, "Help!"

As I took my place opposite these men I realised that some were from the Orthodox church, others were Roman Catholics, and maybe a few were former communists. I needed to win their hearts. I started with a personal story of babysitting for Richard and Mary. One evening when it was time to put Joshua to bed, I kissed him goodnight and said, "What about a prayer, Josh?" I will never forget his reply: "Papa, it's all right; God's in my heart." "Really," I replied, "that's fantastic." He then went on to say, "He is very small and lives right in the corner of my heart and if you want to talk to him it's okay by me." Two weeks later I was with Josh and I asked, "Is God still living in the corner of your heart Josh?" "Oh no Papa," he replied. "He is very big and He is right up to here," and he raised his hands till they were under his chin. It was all very dramatic, and as I told the story to these men I knew I had their attention.

I then unpacked the simple story, saying that prayer starts with a mustard seed of faith (something small in the corner of our heart). Jesus said, "Unless you become like little children ...." All of us are invited by Jesus to pray in faith to God and ask Him into our lives. Without faith it is impossible to please Him. In time He becomes 'very big' in our lives. I then spoke about the cross and what Jesus had done for us. "God so loved the world ...." It was a holy moment and one that I would never forget. Who knows what was the outcome of these meetings? Sitting in the plane on my way home I reflected on these amazing events. What a privilege it had been. Charles Slagel, you did hear from God.

Chapter 23

Special People, Special Lives

Baptisms were times of great celebration, with scores of happy friends crammed around the pool. Nervous but excited young people spoke of their new-found faith and a huge cheer always went up as they went under the water.

The first person to be baptised in the new pool was Pauline Allen, who lived in the apartments opposite the mission. She helped organise the children's playschemes in the mission but never came on a Sunday. Ruth plucked up courage one day and asked her to come. To her surprise she said, "I'll be there." Her faith that had been in a deep freeze for years suddenly thawed out. Because of her love of dancing she started a tap-dancing club for the kids in the area.

I have got to mention Black Doris (she wouldn't mind me referring to her in this way). She was one of the many elderly people picked up by minivan every Sunday. She always said the same thing to me: "That was a good word this morning, Mr. Powell." She was the only person who called me Mr. Powell. We always shook hands – no kissing for Doris.

And there was Sister Winnie Clout, who was greatly loved

by all of us. What a woman! She had lived in Battersea all her life. She wanted to be a schoolteacher, but her father was unable to pay the college fees. She was previously a member of the Zion Mission in Battersea Park Road. She wore a dark blue coat and beret and a brass lapel badge saying 'Deaconess'. This title was only given to someone after conducting the required number of home and hospital visitations, open air services and Sunday school classes. She told me that her ministry was to 'fill the gaps'. If there was a need, she would offer to fill it. Putting out chairs, Sunday school teaching, visiting, preaching, making tea, and much more. This she did from her teenage years till joining us in the mission in her seventies. It was a great privilege to welcome her after the 'Old Zion' was demolished. She loved the children in the mission. Every Sunday she produced a jar full of lollipops. I am not sure if the mothers approved but the children certainly did and made a beeline for her after the closing hymn. One of her greatest joys was to ask our family to dinner on a Sunday. Our three children knew they were in for a feast and she enjoyed piling the food onto their plates. She was a saint.

One day a young mother came to tell the story of her childhood days. It wasn't a happy one; she sobbed as she told it to Anne and Ruth. The friendship grew, trust was established, and in time God healed her of many hurts. She had a lot to forgive. The time came when she asked God to fill her with his love. Everyone looked on in amazement as she fell to her knees, and between gasps she tried to explain what was going on. "The room is filling with a brilliant light," she said. "It's too much." Then came both laughter and tears. "This is so good!" she gasped. She tried closing her eyes to shut the light out, but the light didn't fade. She repeatedly closed her eyes to shut it out. All the time she was saying, "This is amazing!" Ruth did not know what was happening; she couldn't see any light. The time came for her to leave the house. Her final request was, "Do you have any sunglasses? I cannot drive home in safety with this brightness surrounding me." Apparently the light continued to shine on her for days. This lady subsequently did a fantastic job in running a young girls' club in the mission; the children just loved her.

We spread our blankets on the ground, opened our picnic baskets and soon sixty hungry adults and children piled into salads and pop. This was our annual mission outing. This time it was Bushy Park, just a stone's throw from the River Thames. In previous years, we had visited Box Hill, Chessington Zoo and Hyde Park. Everyone agreed that Bushy Park would be great for seven-a-side football and a visit to Hampton Court. It was ideal in every way, with slides and swings for the children, plenty of space for games, and the forecast was for fine weather. It was going to be a fun time.

I don't know who made the challenge but someone shouted "Who will be the first to the top of the chestnut tree?" As a lad I had spent a considerable amount of time climbing trees in the grounds of the manor house opposite our home in Poplar Grove. This was my moment to show the way. Up and up I went; it was just like the old days. Sooner than I realised I was at the top, some sixty feet above ground. The view was terrific. Below me were a dozen men bouncing on the branches having fun. Cameras came out as wives captured them in their wacky poses. Some wives were not so impressed. "For goodness sake, be careful," said one. "Hang on," said another. All the children wanted a bunk up to the lower branches to join their fathers. It really was a very noisy time. Some men remembered their childhood days just as I did. Suddenly we heard a blast on a whistle and then silence. Looking down through the thick branches I could see a policeman standing there with arms folded. Looking very serious he said, "okay, you lot, come down. The fun's over. You should be ashamed of yourselves." Slowly, quietly, everyone else made their way down. However, I was convinced he couldn't see me hidden by the leaves at the top, so I climbed a little higher. I was not going to be humiliated like the rest. Again silence from below as now the subdued mission party were given a lecture on Park regulations. "Great." I thought. "He hasn't seen me and I can come down triumphantly when he has gone." I began to enjoy the view, I could see Hampton Court Palace, and the pond in the centre of the road nearby. Unfortunately this eagle-eyed policeman suddenly spotted me. "Oi, you can come down too," he called out. This was his moment of triumph. I slowly made my way down. As I was about the leap from the final branch to the ground he made a typical schoolteacher's remark: "So you think it's funny, do you?" Up to this time the rest of our party had listened to his lecture in silence, but now, they could restrain themselves no longer; the entire group erupted in laughter. What a sight! Here was I, the pastor, caught up a tree thinking I could outwit the law and then being told that I was a 'naughty boy'. This incident was the highlight of a never-to-be-forgotten day and would no doubt feature in sermons to come. I wonder if the crowd had as big a laugh when Zacchaeus made his final leap from the tree. I wish I had been there.

Chapter 24

The End is Nigh

Over the years we had run several Alpha courses and through the kind offer of Pip and Harry Goring we had arranged to do the 'Holy Spirit Weekend' in their home at Wiston Park House near Worthing. Their house was large enough to take our group of sixteen, although four men had to sleep in one of their small cottages. Harry was amused when these grown men appeared rather worried when he left them late at night in one of his remote cottages. "How do we lock the door when you have gone?" they had asked him. He had a good chuckle about this. It was very kind of them to accommodate our group in their home. Pip could see that Ruth was looking tired and told her that she would be responsible for the catering and Ruth should take it easy. They were familiar with the Alpha course as they had come to renewed faith through it and were involved in the ministry at Holy Trinity Brompton, in London. The weather was perfect and everyone was thrilled to be in this glorious setting in the Sussex Downs. The views from the garden were outstanding – such a contrast from the crowded Doddington Estate in Battersea.

With such a lovely couple caring for us, a wonderful location, great meals, a lot of fun and most importantly, everyone waiting to hear what the Holy Spirit had to say, we were set for a blessed time. We had enjoyed the video talks given by Nicky Gumbel; but now it was time to listen to the Holy Spirit. As the weekend went by it became obvious that several in the group had been touched by the Holy Spirit. We were encouraged to share our experiences and pray together.

Roy, a Battersea man from birth, was part of the group. Since his conversion he had been physically and mentally bullied at work. At one point they placed a cross in the work yard, forced him to lay on it and abused him. The ridicule lasted several weeks till finally he was admitted to hospital exhausted by this constant abuse. I had a huge admiration for him – he was one of the few older local men that became Christians during our time in Battersea.

We came to the final meeting. Roy walked across to Harry who was standing beneath one of the many huge oil paintings in the grand dining room. Placing his hand on Harry's shoulder he said, "'Arry I've got a word for ya." Harry looked a little unsure, wondering what he was going to hear. Roy continued. "And what is more, 'Arry, I'm gonna sing it to ya." My thoughts just raced at this point, for he was no soloist, and, as far as I knew he had never given a prophecy before. Here he was standing beside a gentleman farmer whose land covered 6,000 acres of beautiful Sussex Downs. I need not have worried. It was a wonderful 'God moment'. Roy, led in the Spirit, spoke about the manor house they owned and how God was going to use it in the years to come. At that time neither Roy nor I had any idea that estate would one day host 'The Big Church Day Out'. When he finished they hugged each other and Harry's face was wet with tears, as were many other faces in the room.

So the weekend drew to a close but not before Pip took Ruth aside and said that she had something to say to her. Sitting together in a quiet room she said to Ruth that she believed our time in Battersea was coming to an end and we should prepare for the future and move on. Not long after, this was confirmed by Jo Watts' father. When I talked to Jo afterwards, she said, "You had better take notice of that; dad never says something of that importance unless he thinks it's from God."

I've named this book 'Get A Life'. I had to accept that our time in Battersea was coming to an end. Twenty-seven years had seen 'the sparrow fall to ground' just as Jesus said. Mistakes had been made, but thankfully He always picked us up and we flew on again. We had certainly been through a lot of dramatic in-flight experiences which would never be forgotten. So what next? I was coming up to sixty-five and retirement. With so many of the family overseas the obvious thing would be to plan a round-the-world trip and see the homes and families we had heard about for so many years. The first stop was Long Island in the USA, the new home of my sister Jennifer. She had just moved there to be with her two children Lorna and Bruce and her five grandchildren. The weather was hot and humid. The location was beautiful and the visits we went on with her in the surrounding area were most memorable. We will never forget the time we ate corn on the cob soaked in butter on Pumpkin Day. Smithtown Tabernacle and their fun-loving Pastor Forseth and his flamboyant family will remain in our memories, as will the golden beaches and exciting visits to the 'Big Apple'.

We had a great time with Jennifer. The next stop was Havelock North in New Zealand. This was a visit we had planned ever since Ruth's parents emigrated there forty-five years ago. By now they had long since returned to England, but Ruth was keen to see all the places she had heard about from her parents. After a long search we finally found the house her father had lovingly built. To our relief, the present owner was delighted to hear our story and immediately invited us in. Ruth's emotions ran high as we went from room to room. If only we could have visited them when they were living there. Her father often told us about the lemon tree in the garden. Apparently he had a glass of fresh lemon juice every day before breakfast. The new owners allowed us to pick one to take home to him. Our final visit was to Madeline and Ray in Vancouver. This was our first visit to beautiful BC. The city lived up to its name with its fantastic mountain ranges looking down on huge expanses of water surrounding the city. Luxury liners waited to take passengers to Alaska, while seaplanes came and went just a few yards from the shoreline. There were high-rise apartments situated right at the water's edge and so much more. But above all, it was good to be in Madeline's home and enjoy meals together. She and Ray had left England forty-five years ago and apart from a few welcome visits, we had seen very little of each other since. Our stay included a whirlwind tour visiting her children Michelle, Andrea and Michael and her four grandchildren. Too soon our long-awaited trip was over. We had been with loved ones, visited beautiful countries, and looked with a certain amount of envy at the amazing homes built on the rocky shores of Canada. The taxi ride from Victoria to Battersea only took a few minutes and although it was good to pull up outside our own home, we both looked at each other in dismay as the taxi pulled away and left us in a road covered in litter. I don't think we said anything but our thoughts were one. "Oh dear, dear, dear, what a contrast. Come on, let's go in and have a proper cup of tea."

We had no intention of selling our house for a year or two but I felt it would be helpful if we could get some idea of its value. I called the local estate agent and arranged for him to visit. He was most impressed with the property, and so he should be, for I had worked hard to improve it in every way. We had built a conservatory at the back, a porch on the front which included a toilet and washbasin and a fantastic loft extension, most of which I had done myself. As a parting remark he said, "Why not put it on the market now, see if anyone is interested?" He was a good salesman. Without too much thought, I agreed. That was on the Friday. On the following Monday I spent the day at the Oval cricket ground watching the West Indies get soundly beaten. On my return home Ruth greeted me with the astonishing news that she had sold the house. My immediate reaction was, "Oh no!" and I collapsed on the sofa. My thoughts were racing. I was just speechless, but Ruth's next comment was even more threatening: "They want to move in straight away." Apparently the would-be purchaser said they wanted the house for their son and were prepared to write out a cheque for it on the spot. Needless to say, that evening we spent hours coming to terms with the unexpected development. The question was, "Where do we go from here?" It was all very well wanting to move at some time in the future but now the future had suddenly arrived.

Ruth was a Sussex girl, so why not return to her county? The Goring family lived in Sussex and had made us very welcome during the Alpha course. Maybe we should explore that part of the country. Hasty phone calls were made and once again they kindly said they had a week when we could use their house. This was so kind of them, and to add to the pleasure they explained where the key for the swimming pool was kept. Also the fridge was full of food waiting to be eaten. We have been friendly with them ever since and have shared in the vision of Wiston House becoming a House of Prayer.

For a week Jenny, Ruth and I explored the local villages. It wasn't until the last day, when our hopes of finding a suitable property had faded, that we were directed to a delightful bungalow called 'Evergreen' in Ivy Lane, Ashington. Immediately we all thought, "Wow!" Set in a third of an acre at the end of a private lane with a small woodland only a few yards away, this was our country ranch. The lounge was thirty feet long with glorious French doors opening onto a garden just full of potential. It had two huge bedrooms and a third smaller room. The whole place was looking a little tired but that didn't matter, as DIY was something I enjoyed. The asking price was £3,000 more than we could afford. Apparently it should have been on the market for much more. The estate manager was upset about this, but the client wanted a quick sale. Our offer was accepted and we returned home in a state of shock. It was hard to believe that for an extra £3,000, we could swap our ex-council house with two thousand trains a day rumbling past the end of our garden for a ranch in the country.

The twenty-seven years in Battersea had come to a close. Ruth and the family sat with me on the mission platform looking at the hundreds of friends who had come not only to say farewell, but to celebrate together the rich life we had experienced at the Shaftesbury Christian Centre. Each one had a story to tell. Some were with us for a lifetime, some for several years, while others just passed through. Yet all had contributed to the life of faith in the inner city. Many have moved on – some to the USA, others to Canada, Australia, Africa, Turkey, Jersey, Wales, Scotland, Spain, the South of France, Tasmania and the Shetland Isles. Some had moved to St Mark's, Battersea Rise, a popular local Anglican church. The leadership team had also moved on, with Anne and Geoff moving to Torquay in Devon, Mick and Theresa to Weymouth, Dorset and Colin and Debbie to Bosham, Sussex. A good friend of ours used to say, "Constant change is here to stay." How true that is; nothing is really settled in life. However, true friends are forever and we are so blessed that Brian and Jo who are the pastors at the mission give all of us such a tremendous welcome every time we enter the building.

Some time after the 'farewell/reunion' Ruth and I attended a party at the mission. Ruth was dressed as 'Little Bo Peep' and carried a shepherd's staff. We had bought it years ago in the Shetland Isles. We had a great time that night. We always did. Mission people were good at parties. The evening came to a close, and I found Brian in the kitchen with a dishcloth in his hand. I had the shepherd's staff in my hand. It was one of those 'God moments'. Hearing me come into the kitchen, he turned to me with a smile and said, "Another good evening, Tony." I intended saying,

"Goodbye, it's been a great party," and bid him farewell but something more important came to mind. I had to give him the shepherd's staff. Why? Because it's a symbol of leadership. It wasn't planned, and everything happened so quickly. I didn't need to say anything; it wasn't necessary. We both recognised the symbol in my hand. This was a divine appointment. I simply said, "It's yours, Brian." We both knew the staff confirmed his calling to lead. It truly was a 'God moment'. He put the dishcloth down on the table and took the staff with tears saying, "You will never know what this means to me." My thoughts went back to the kitchen table in the mission house all those years ago. God now had fresh new plans for the mission. We left the building that night and made our way home to our 'ranch' knowing the life of the mission was in good hands. In fact in very, very good hands.

Thank you Jesus.

If you want to contact Tony and Ruth our email address is evergreen8@btinternet.com or write c/o The Shaftesbury Christian Centre, Austin Road, Battersea, London SW11 5JP